What's Money Got to Do with It?

Learn to change your money story, mindset, and improve your financial future

Compiled by Heather Andrews

Gratitude

First, I want to thank each of the co-authors that contributed to this book for their vulnerability and willingness to share their knowledge. Their stories are powerful, and their wisdom will offer you the path to changing your financial story.

I am grateful to my amazing, publishing team: my editors who help guide and coach our authors through the process of sharing their stories despite their fears. My graphic design team who created the cover and my podcast team for helping our co-authors bring a voice to their story.

I am grateful to you, our readers. Thank you for joining our journey.

Most of all, I am grateful for the lessons I have learned through my finance story. I am glad we are finally bringing the topic of money to the table so we as a society can openly discuss, learn, and grow together for a stronger financial future for ourselves and our community.

Hugs,
Heather

Contents

Foreword

Jay Tsougrianis

Simply put, money is a fact of life.

It's a word that has multiple facets and causes emotions that range from one end of the spectrum to the other. It can be the cause of happiness and joy when one uses it to share gifts, go on a vacation, or have dinner with loved ones. It can be used for good: to make donations or raise funds for a charity or help someone get back on their feet. When money is used in a positive way, it brings out feelings of gratitude, hope and kindness.

Then there is the other side of money, the side the brings out the worst in people. When we have a negative relationship with money it causes significant greed and anxiety, it divides families, businesses, communities and countries. It is the cause of hatred, crime, dishonesty — even war.

The one fact that remains though is that money is a basic necessity. We all need food, shelter, water and clothing. Therefore, we need money to survive. How then do we develop a healthy relationship to money when we all need it? How do we move from a mentality of scarcity and competition, to one of abundance?

When I finally developed a healthy relationship to money and my possessions everything changed. I used to look at money as a means to an end. The harder I worked the more I earned, the more I bought, the more I had. I would do whatever it took to earn more money, so I could buy more things, and portray an image of "having it all." Sadly, I realized that the image on the outside was far from the reality on the inside. The desire to be rich had broken me and I was working in jobs that were misaligned with my core values. I was held there by the golden handcuffs, the promise of more, and the belief that as my pay increased, so would my happiness.

My purpose is not to declare money as a bad thing. You see I have come to understand that when I align my core values with my desire to earn money, my entire perspective changes. For me money is no longer about having things, but about discovering my gifts so I may share them with others, empowering those people as well. It is about finding freedom: freedom from worry, freedom from competition, freedom from possessions, and most importantly freedom from the opinions of others. When I lived my life chasing a certain lifestyle that I believed would make me happy, the exact opposite happened. I began to hate my life, I was tired of being someone else, and tired of trying to impress upon others how successful I was.

I now think of my relationship with money as one small part of the whole. There are so many areas of our lives that we give up in the pursuit of financial rewards, and sadly, we define ourselves on the basis of achieving them. The real question is, what is life without balance? When we make life solely about money, the other parts of our life suffer. What I've come to realize is that no matter how much money I have, it won't matter if I am divorced, my kids hate me, my friends and community have given up on me and my physical and emotional health is failing.

In the west we are programmed to believe that balance is a fallacy, and that the only way to achieve balance is to retire rich. Have you ever heard someone say, "When I am rich and retire, I will have time to look after my health, I will have time to contribute, and I will have time to enjoy my friends and family?"

I hate to be the bearer of bad news, but a lifetime of self-abuse and neglect of your relationships and health will not turn around the moment you retire. All too often we are reminded by this truth when a friend or family member has died from some preventable disease. If only they had taken the time to look after their health when they were younger. Or that rich old executive, who has long been divorced, paying exorbitant child and spousal support to the spouse they neglected to make time for when they were married.

Now I'm not saying, sit back, relax and coast at work, and everything will be fine financially. From experience I know that hard work is a must and having a good career takes skill and commitment. What I am saying is don't forget why you are working as hard as you are. Don't forget that there is more to life than work and money. Your gravestone likely won't be adorned by the number of digits you had in your bank account. People might remember you for how much money you had, but they are more likely to remember how you treated them, how you loved, and how you added value to the world.

Learn to respect yourself and others, educate yourself about money, but also and more importantly in matters of the heart. Last but not least, learn to live with authenticity, give fully of yourself and learn the art of gratitude. What we focus on grows, so focus on what you want out of life, focus on abundance, your health, your family and today. Ask yourself often, "what can I start doing right now that will add abundance in all areas of my life?"

No matter how many millions you have or don't have, your relationship with money is a choice. It is never too late to sit down and chart out what really matters most for you and your family. Be grateful for what you will learn in this book, as each author brings with them an immense amount of life experience and helpful suggestions. Use this opportunity as a starting point to re-evaluate what is most important to you in your life. Only you can decide whether you control money or money controls you.

I am grateful to my mother and father who raised me to be open, honest and hard working.

To my husband and children, who have stuck with me through thick and thin, when my job and drive for money was so strong that I ignored all the important parts of my life, thank you.

Thank you to Heather and her team at Follow it Thru for inviting me to be one of the authors in this project. I am excited for the future and I am honored to work alongside such visionaries.

Introduction

I was raised with the belief that the harder, longer and better I worked, the more money I would make. It was guaranteed. And the more money I made, the more I would be 'worth.'

Sounds like a winning formula for a successful life, doesn't it? A simple algorithm to achieve the 'American dream' of a comfortable, stress-free life—*piece of cake.*

The last few years have taught me that financial success is anything *but* guaranteed and even more difficult when you choose to follow an entrepreneurial path.

I was devasted when my lifelong career in healthcare management was turned upside down in June 2015; 'restructured' into an unknown world of doubt, fear and financial scarcity. *It was perfect.*

Little did I know then, but that juncture would be the impetus for a total change in direction, and is inevitably the reason you are holding this book in your hand today. In June 2017, my first compilation book, *Obstacles Equal Opportunities,* launched on Amazon. The publishing division of my coaching company was born, and has subsequently grown into my own brand of Heather Andrews and Follow It Thru Publishing. I am thrilled to say the stage is already set for 2019 and our team has *tripled* in size.

Being an entrepreneur has undoubtedly tempered me into a stronger, wiser version of myself. It has taught me to get up and get after it, even when I don't feel like it. It has shown me I am worthy of more, and that I am capable of creating more, for myself and for those on this path with me.

It has made me richer, although not necessarily monetarily (yet). It has made me question the differences between money, value, and worth; and how we often mistakenly tie our self-worth to our financial well-being, our careers, and to climbing that rickety, over-burdened corporate ladder.

'Success' simply cannot be judged by bank balance alone.

As the idea for this new compilation grew, so did the list of co-authors eager to come on board, all willing to share their personal stories about their own relationships with money, and the lessons they've learned along the way.

Collectively, we hope you are able to find wisdom and solace in the sharing of our experiences, in our lessons learned, and in the mindset tips from each co-author.

Pursue your dreams; the money will follow. Let us help you on your own path, whatever direction it may lead.

Love,
Heather

Mike Skrypnek

Mike is recognized as Canada's leading authority and coach for business growth and entrepreneurial freedom. He is an accomplished author of six books on giving and business success and a speaker who has delivered hundreds of motivating presentations by sharing his Grow, Get, Give philosophy with thousands of entrepreneurs.

Mike's quick learning style and innovative marketing ideas enabled him to grow (and sell) a dominant niche financial advisory business focusing on helping others give. Importantly, he has helped guide entrepreneurs and affluent families redirect $12.5 million in Big Impact Giving since 2012. As an expert coach, his attention is focused on helping entrepreneurs **grow** their business, **get** more freedom and **give** back.

Entrepreneurs seek freedom. Freedom is measured in time, money, energy, and impact. Mike is your ultimate business guide to entrepreneurial freedom.

Connect with Mike:

info@MikeSkrypnek.com

From Scarcity to Abundance

An Expert Opinion by Mike Skrypnek

I grew up in Calgary, Alberta, in a low-income neighborhood with drug dealers, thieves, bike gangs, and many impoverished people. The neighborhood was littered with 50s styled homes and subsidized housing. Our little brown house with the white picket fence was wedged between the TransCanada Highway and another major thoroughfare. This transient community was our playground, our home. We had a bird's eye view of the most interesting scenes you could imagine. I always said if we were living in the U.S.A, there would have been gun shots and crack dealers all around us. Fortunately, that dynamic simply did not exist at the time…or I might not be writing my story right now.

There is a saying though, about how 'a dog won't shit in its own backyard'. Our thieves would go to other neighborhoods to steal—they had better stuff. What were they going to steal from their poor neighbors? While our environment was dysfunctional, that was not the case in our white picket oasis. Growing up, there was an immense amount of love and care within our house. My parents had convinced my sister, Cheryl, and I that we were middle class. Maybe we were middle class in Montgomery, but we certainly not on a wider scale in an affluent business-friendly city. It sure did feel middle class, though. We never noticed if we went without. We got what we needed (Foot Locker brand and not Nike, sometimes secondhand rather than new) and we had access to sports teams, music, and activities—enough to keep us busy. Hobbies like golf or skiing were never options, and family vacations were always within a few hours' drive.

There were a lot of kids in the hood, so we had plenty to do. During the 70s, parents would simply show you the door in the morning—in fact they would typically kick you outside—and expect that you were within earshot of the *"lunch"* or *"dinner"* call Mom would yell from the top of the front porch. If you could hear her, no matter how faint, you were close enough.

Growing up biking and playing football, volleyball, basketball, and road hockey with my friends led us to believe we were all the same. It was only as I became an adult and attended university that I realized that the other kids in my neighborhood weren't as fortunate as us. Equally so, I came to the realization that others had a much different, more affluent life than ours. Our neighbors had their own myriad of problems, ranging from poverty to abuse to lack of parenting. You name it; they faced it. When I got older, I wanted to be sure to give back whenever I could. It mattered to me to give back to the community that helped me grow up. To help kids and families that didn't have the quality of life or opportunity I was fortunate enough to have grown up with meant everything to me.

My dad grew up just down the block from our family home, and my grandparents lived there while I was young. My mom grew up only a few blocks away too. I always thought it was strange that my parents did not know each other before they fell in love in their late teens. They could have practically seen each other's homes from their own back yards. It was only after grade school that they met, introduced by mutual friends in the same neighborhood (go figure).

Both of my parents worked very hard. When it came to their jobs, they often created success in the face of adversity. My dad was an intelligent person, but he was held back by mental illness. The consensus diagnosis was schizophrenia. As far as I was concerned, he was always a functioning and 'normal' man. When I attended university, I asked my dad what it was like for him at my age when he was hospitalized with his illness. He simply answered that it was exactly like the movie *One Flew Over the Cuckoo's Nest*, only with more shock treatments. He is convinced the treatments are the reason he is alive today. We were fortunate with Dad that his illness was not a delusional, paranoia-filled madness. With medication, he was quite functional.

My mom is an amazing person. She left home when she was only sixteen. To her lifelong friends and people who meet her, she is one of the most caring, genuinely decent people that ever walked the earth. Without her, my dad would have returned to the hospital numerous times, ended up on the streets, or taking his own life. When they met, it was true love. They formed an immediate bond, and she faithfully stuck with him as he found his way to (medically controlled) sanity. In 1968, they were married, and in 1970 I was born.

Fast forward to the '80s. The oil and gas-fueled city of Calgary was reeling from an energy crisis, and more pain would follow. The '70s were a hangover from the free love 60s. At the time, there was a new government initiative called the National Energy Program founded by the first Trudeau government. The goal was security of supply and ultimate independence from the world oil market. An opportunity was given to participate in the energy industry and a revenue-sharing regime which recognized the needs and rights of all Canadians.

That 'revenue-sharing' was double taxation for Alberta oil producers. The 'Robin Hood' program took money directly from Albertans and redistributed to other provinces. Inflation and double-digit interest rates crushed Alberta's oil industry. The program had the complete opposite effect than intended. The NEP opened offices in Calgary as oil businesses were still suffering. Job losses were staggering, and people who were being crushed under the weight of their mortgages simply gave their keys back to the bank.

Through it all, my parents managed to keep our little brown house with the white picket fence on the corner. My mom worked as an aid in an elementary school, and my dad had worked as a draftsman for Union 76 and as a salesman of drafting supplies and equipment to the oil and gas industry for a company called Caldraft. He was a great salesman, but nothing about the social demands of sales came naturally to him. He joined Toastmasters and would rehearse his pitch and speeches in front of the hall mirror in our tiny kitchen night after night. However, no family was left untouched by the downturn, and it didn't take long for my dad to lose his job serving the oil patch.

Desperation breeds ingenuity and action. My dad took many jobs he didn't like or couldn't handle just to keep the bills paid. At the time, a new three-story building had been built along the TransCanada Highway across from where we lived. It was the largest new building in the community for a long time. My dad quickly contacted the building owners and somehow landed a property management role. He was creative, and it certainly paid off. This was the beginning of his entrepreneurship and self-employment. He refused to let his fate lie in anyone else's hands.

There was a great side effect of my dad's new role: he always needed extra help. The type of help that my teenage soccer teammates and I could provide. We all liked having a little extra money, so we mowed and landscaped lawns, shoveled snow, did demolition and construction, and anything else a building with many tenants would need.

One of my most consistent jobs for a couple years, while I was in junior high school, was cleaning. I would clean offices Tuesday, Thursday, and Sunday nights. This involved vacuuming, emptying the garbage, and cleaning the bathrooms. It was okay, but I didn't care much since the pay kept funding my Slurpee's needs and extra wants, like saving for my first car.

What I didn't know then, that I learned many years later, was that the primary tenant of the building was the NEP. What painful, bittersweet irony it must have been for my father. He had work, but it was cleaning the garbage and toilets of the NEP. The very program that put him (and thousands of Calgarians) out of work.

That was just the beginning of my father's self-employment. He parlayed this role into other jobs and was able to save some money and pay off debts. He spent time looking for a simple, blue collar business that he could run without having too much human interaction. He first bought an aerial bucket truck and did sign installations, lighting, and anything else you could imagine that required taking something from ground level and raising it up thirty feet. He even found some work in the movie industry on a semi-regular basis. He was able to grow his business, and it served our family well for about five years. The business was stable, but it depended heavily on him hustling all the time to make sales, so he started to look for something with a bit more consistency.

Shortly after, he identified and bought a portable sign company. This seemed to fit nicely with his business, and he already had the truck that was needed to haul the large, hulking signs to their destination. There was a better level of repeat and multi-month contracts (in some cases multi-year) that smoothed out the revenue for him. All the work he had built for himself was labor intensive, but I helped out regularly, and he hired part-time help, too. Things were going okay, and my mother soon left her position with the school board to help my dad run the business. She handled all the office work, customer relationships, and collections. She also put the marketing message orders together so he could take them out and place them in the sign. Of course, they learned this through trial and error. No one ever told them *how*. They bought the business and learned everything from scratch. There was no policy manual, and no procedures were explained. Dad simply went out a few times with the previous owner and that was all the training he received. After that, he arranged a loan with the bank and bought the company.

There was an art to the business, and a process was needed. The words had to be spelled out, organized, and the plastic ten-inch letters had to be compiled and placed in milk crates in the reverse order so that my dad could pull them out and place them on the signs correctly. My parents worked well together, but this was a twelve to fourteen hour a day gig, six to seven days per week. It was hard work, especially in -20-degree weather. As tough as the work was, it seemed to suit my parents just fine. They were their own bosses and had no one to answer to except for themselves and their customers.

For a decade, this seemed to work quite well. Self-employment had given my parents the freedom to earn what they could, rely only on themselves, and manage their hours and their workload as they wanted. The only problem was that they bought into their own jobs and never seemed to stop working. The idea of being business *owners* with *freedom* from their jobs simply did not materialize.

They weren't disappointed; they just didn't know what they didn't know. They lacked the skills, knowledge, and mentorship to guide them to the next level. They seemed happy and didn't stress about bills too much. Our parents loved my sister and me, and that's what was most important.

The lessons I learned from my parents in business were:

- Work hard.

- People will let you down.

- Trust only in yourself and your family.

- Earn money.

- Spend money.

- Pay your rent/mortgage.

- If you needed more money, work harder doing whatever you can.

- Trade time for money.

- Build a life that is good enough.

- And most importantly - keep moving forward.

My education around money was to avoid anything that cost too much. I limited my educational goals to what I could pay for with scholarships, my summer jobs, and student loans. I wanted to go to the U.S.A to advance my education, but it was very expensive. I didn't consider that to borrow for it would result in a better role and, ultimately, a better ability to pay back a loan. They also (subconsciously I'm sure) taught me that if you can't afford something, don't do it. It was a scarcity mentality. I had an abundance of personal confidence (often borne out of fiscal naivety) but a mindset that saw ceilings and limits to financial growth or opportunity. Big dreams, but 'right-sized'.

My dad might have thought he was expanding and diversifying, but really, he was scrambling to increase his income. They never hired help. There was no manager, no part-time employees, and no proper systems in place. They simply made things up as they went along. They had a process, but it was built on necessity, not strategy.

I entered the workforce with a good work ethic but had no idea about saving, investing, P&L, accounting, how taxes worked, or how money can change people. Early on, I traded time for money, but I soon grew weary.

I built Western Canada's largest personal training agency and had others earning *for me*. However, since I didn't understand how the business worked, I worked to pay all the bills, then invested the trainers' future (unearned) revenue in marketing and sales. I was spending money I didn't have with uneducated attempts to increase sales but forgot to train my consultants on how to sell and serve *their* customers. If I didn't do the training myself, the company wouldn't survive. I went about running a business in all the wrong ways—just like my parents.

Working twenty hours per day soon caught up with me. I grew exhausted of the treadmill I put myself on and had contempt for my employees.

During that time, I was offered a job in the investment industry, with the promise of unlimited money for a limited time. I jumped at the offer. In the early days, it seemed that the promise was legitimate. I could earn more money than I ever imagined simply by convincing people to invest in companies that my senior advisor supported. In the mid-90s, commissions were high, and the job seemed easy. Just sell. I knew nothing about the investment industry and had no training other than a course required to acquire my license. I learned nothing, and the money was easy…until it was gone.

In 1997, a couple of things happened. First, another oil price shock drove the Calgary markets down as prices dropped by 60% in a month. All the focus of my investment business was on oil stocks, which had risen precipitously in the years prior. My naïve idea of portfolio diversification was that you owned a large company, a medium company, small companies, and some venture companies—all related to oil and gas. These were 'learned' behaviors. I knew nothing about investing.

Then came the largest tax bill I had ever received—and couldn't pay. I had earned more money the year before than ever, but in the current year, business was going badly. In fact, the tax bill was so large that the government threatened to pursue my assets, garnish my wages, and take my first house. I was petrified and didn't know how things worked. Again, no one taught me, so I didn't know how to prepare for this scenario.

So, I sold my first house, liquidated my crippled investments, and paid the tax bill. Afterward, I had enough to at least buy another smaller home. No one told me you could make payment arrangements and that I didn't have to fear for my assets. No one told me that when you owe a large amount of money, the government will work *with* you to help you pay it off. Once again, I approached the situation from a scarcity mindset just like I had witnessed from my parents.

Nearly seven years from the date I started in the investment industry, I took my first *serious* course on the science of investing. (Imagine that.)

Serving people and managing their money while learning things on the fly was not good practice. I decided to patch a lot of holes in my boat. From that point, I took a new course and accreditation every single year. I discovered some extraordinary minds in economics and finance and learned from them. They were Nobel Prize winners and academics. This focus fixed my lack of understanding of how money, investing, and financial markets worked. For the first time, twelve years after I left university, I finally understood a great deal about money.

My new-found knowledge showed in my business and its growth. It showed in my accumulation of wealth and the quality of my decisions. The only thing it didn't do was prepare me for the biggest downturn in markets since the Great Depression.

In 2008, while I had done many things right, I hadn't built a business that could withstand major shock. My lack of preparedness for hard times and my habits of spending money I didn't have struck again. Another big tax bill, followed by another low-income year, investments that were decimated, terrible business partners, and pervasive fear in my industry forced my hand again. I moved to another firm—it felt like I was starting from scratch once more. The difference was this time I had learned a lot, attracted good value for my services at a new firm, and bought myself time to gain the training and education required to build my business the right way.

Even through the market crash and my transition, there were some good things that happened. My clients were positioned to survive through the downturn and thrive on the other side. We had made good decisions on risk and investing. Fortunately, I also had my house. It was valuable enough and had enough equity that I could weather this storm. Lastly, in my move to a new firm, I was compensated, which bought me time. There were many lessons learned, but too many recurring themes. I had to change my situation for *good*.

Finally, I was prepared and aware enough to change. The following ten years would set the stage for a bright future. I had spent most of my life working in the 'greed-is-good' industry, and at that point, I committed to giving $1 million to charity every year. This public commitment and personal pledge set me on a course towards my higher purpose. I didn't have $1 million to give, but I intended to figure it out.

After arising from the worst downturn in history with funds in my bank account and a ton of academic knowledge, I invested in coaching. I had to learn everything I could about how I would reach my philanthropic goals. I hired people who could help me and devoted my energy to becoming an expert in the field of planned-giving. I was on the path to building genuine wisdom. Coaching helped me to learn how to run a serving business, as an *owner*. I had learned tough lessons about money the hard way, and now it was time to understand how to build something —a process—that I could always rely on to make me the money I needed to live and care for my family. In one decade, I invested almost $180,000 into my education, and it paid off. During that time (a six-year period), I had written my first three books on philanthropy and business, helped families redirect over $12.5 million to charitable causes, helped them save over $5 million in taxes, and grew my business tenfold. It was the success of my lifetime.

I learned the following:

- Serve your prospects and customers.
- Work right.
- Become a specialist.
- Be valuable to valuable people.
- Learn how to speak in public.
- Build a mountain of credibility.
- Read.
- Hire coaches.
- Seek great mentors.
- Write books.
- People, processes, and systems will give you time, energy, and freedom.
- Be generous.
- Be grateful.
- Be courageous and confident, not fearful.

I had finally adopted an abundance mindset rather than a scarcity mindset.

In my personal growth and lessons learned around money, I also realized that I was in the investment industry to stay close to money—the money that I never had growing up. Managing money and being connected to investment returns that I had *zero* control over while also being held accountable to every percentage point was the thing I liked *least* about my life. My value to families came in the form of strategic thinking and planning. Connecting a path to people's dreams and vision for the future from where they were was the real benefit. *That* is *real* coaching.

In 2014, I was ready to make the shift that would change my life. My business had a good value, and I was able to strike a deal to sell it, which enabled me to exit the money management industry and expand my problem-solving and coaching role. The course was set for me to focus all my efforts on working as a business coach. I knew what I wanted/needed to do.

My vision was to listen to entrepreneurs and business owners and discover their greatest challenges. I wanted to help them grow their own business, get more freedom, and give back to their communities. I would teach people how to live a life of abundance.

Today, that is exactly what I'm doing. I may have taken the hard roads to get here, but here I am—helping others to avoid those detours and get straight to their destination.

Alana Heim, CPA/PFS, CFP®

Alana Heim (rhymes with Anaheim) has a love for numbers and a passion for creating more value in the world. As the founder of Prosperity Alignment, she uses intuition and strategies to guide you to align and sustain yourself from the inside out, so abundance is a natural occurrence in your life.

Alana's vision is for every person to align with their unique wealth powers so they can positively and powerfully effect change in the world. She is a certified public accountant, a personal financial specialist, a licensed insurance agent, and a Certified Financial Planner™. She is also a certified Human Design specialist, a quantum alignment system practitioner, and an inspirational speaker. She wrote the chapter *Money* in Karen Curry Parker's bestselling book, *Abundance by Design: Discover Your Unique Code for Health, Wealth and Happiness With Human Design.*

Alana, a Projector, lives in Reno, Nevada with her Projector husband and their three children, a Projector daughter, and a set of Generator twins.

Connect with Alana:

info@ProsperityAlignment.com

Chapter 1

Take Control of Your Financial Well-Being

By Alana Heim, CPA/PFS, CFP®

"Take responsibility for your finances or get used to
taking orders for the rest of your life.
You're either a master of money or a slave to it. Your choice."
- Robert T. Kiyosaki

Finance often evokes such negative feelings that you may avoid the topic altogether. It can seem easier to give your financial responsibility to someone else. Someone who will manage your finances for you. But who? I mean, who wants to deal with numbers anyway?

My love for numbers began at a young age. I remember playing a game called Around the World in elementary school. This is a fast-paced game where you go one-on-one against classmates to answer math problems as fast as possible. I could easily go through my entire class (around the world) without losing. I loved the game because I loved math.

In high school, I took five years of math. I had to double up one year so that I could take calculus in my senior year. In calculus, I studied with my teacher so I could sit for the advanced placement exam necessary to earn college credit. As if that wasn't enough, during that same year, I also chose to take an accounting class. What adolescent chooses to take calculus and accounting? This gal.

Based on the above information, you may think I was one of those kids who knew what she wanted to do when she grew up. The truth is I did not know. In fact, I agonized over what to study at university. I knew that most of the schools wanted me to declare a major so I could start on my career path from day one. But I didn't know what that was. So, I went off to college as an undecided major, seeking to learn while feeling determined to land my dream career.

Luckily, the university offered placement tests to guide me. I can still remember one of the career options being an air traffic controller. Yikes. No thanks. Business seemed like a sound choice. I mean, our world is based upon businesses, and businesses deal with numbers. With businesses earning money, and money based upon numbers, it somehow felt…right. Who knew? I fell in love with accounting and chose that degree.

You can imagine my surprise when I shared my love with others, and nearly everyone turned up their noses and told me what an awful choice I made. "*Ugh*," they would cry out. "I can't *stand* accounting. That's why I chose finance." It made me feel nervous to share this love, so I slowly and quietly began keeping my feelings a secret. I didn't have the awareness to see the gift I possessed. I began keeping my gift hidden inside of me.

I carried my love for numbers into my first accounting internship position. I was blessed to have a college professor invite me to interview with an accounting firm which would go on to hire me permanently within that first year. I was overjoyed to be on my career path—a path that I didn't know I would find when I left for college. There I was, twenty years old, loving my new career, loving numbers, and loving life.

Approximately seven years later, I experienced age discrimination for the first time. Although I did look young for my age, I was already married, with seven years of tax and accounting experience under my belt.

An older woman of about fifty came in as a new potential client. The partners and managers had directed her to meet with me. I led her back to my office where my certified public accountant certificate, Certified Financial Planner™ certificate, and Master of Accountancy diploma hung on the wall.

As we sat down, I began to engage with her. I asked her questions about the support she needed with preparing her income tax return. As I continued to inquire, I suddenly felt the heaviness from within her cascade into the room. The energy shift was so intense that my confidence began to wane. I felt nervous and inadequate.

With disdain in her voice and on her face, she cut me off and demanded that I was "too young" to work with her. My voice wavered as I attempted to assure her I had more than enough experience. I could feel my face flush. I hadn't expected discrimination, nor had I experienced it before. I was in shock that somehow the numbers were against me. The numbers I loved so much were suddenly not on my side as a "young" CPA.

It didn't matter what I said. She had made her choice. She wanted to work with someone else because she believed I was too young and lacked experience. She didn't see the value that I could bring. She didn't trust *me*.

As she left my office, I realized that her energy had influenced the numbers against me in a negative way. At that moment, fear set in that I wasn't good enough. My love and passion for my work were not enough to serve her. Sadly, my self-worth and love for numbers dimmed a little that day.

When it comes to money and finances, this is just one of the stigmas. You want to work with somebody who has financial expertise. You may want someone who understands you and your needs, but often you want them to be 'old enough'. If someone is young, they're not good enough.

In reverse, I've seen older mentors work themselves out of a job due to their age. They may have reached retirement age, but often they were urged to make the choice to leave as their sharpness may have dulled.

As a client, it can feel like a real dilemma wondering what kind of financial professional to choose. Do you choose someone who is young and maybe not as experienced? Or do you choose the older wiser professional who has been in the industry for up to fifty years?

This is where we feel our fears surface. If you do not work with anyone on your finances, fears can arise around not having enough money to warrant the support. If you do have an advisor, fears can come up about trusting them with your money. When you *do* trust them, you may fear what will happen should they pass away. Where will you find a new expert? What expertise and knowledge should you seek to help you manage your money for you? Who will serve you?

This is the real crux of the fear. *Who will manage your finances for you?*

Having served in the financial industry for nearly twenty years, I have realized that not everyone enjoys having financial responsibility. It is why people balked at my career choice. It is why you may worry about budgeting, balancing checking accounts, and doing math. It is why it can feel easier to hand over your money to a professional. Out of sight, out of mind.

My clients feared not knowing *how* to be responsible. Many were good at their work, but they worried about managing their money. Usually, these fears stemmed from past experiences where they made mistakes, weren't good with numbers or witnessed their parents struggle financially.

Although I have a love of numbers and enjoy managing my finances, I am by no means perfect. Financially, I did what I believed was right. Yes, I believed in saving and being financially responsible. It's probably why this career fits me. I have experienced financial ups and downs. For example, I made over six figures on my first home purchase…only to turn around and put that right back in my second home, which ended up declining in value during the real estate bubble.

Then I went through a divorce. The bank was unwilling to refinance the loan into my name, which would have left me and my ex holding joint ownership—something I didn't want. So, to walk away, I made the tough decision of short-selling the home. That meant I couldn't hold on to the home to ride out the bubble and get my money back. Unfortunately, I lost a lot of money—from the divorce and the short-sell. Was it a poor choice? No. It was a good learning experience for which I am grateful.

Would it be easier if someone else took care of your financial responsibilities on your behalf? Would it give you peace of mind to let someone else manage those responsibilities? Or would it weaken the control you have over your own life and your financial well-being?

I encourage you to ask yourself if this belief is true. It is easy to think that it is best to give away your power, and to go along with what society tells you is best. However, it may be difficult to decide which financial professional to choose.

Here is a quick example:

Imagine you are walking down the street. It is a bright and beautiful day to get your finances in order. You know you need financial guidance and are open to learning and exploring options but are unsure of the support you need.

As you turn your head and look across the street, you notice two storefronts next to each other. You start to cross the street. On one door, it says 'FINANCIAL ADVISOR'. On the other door, it says 'INSURANCE AGENT'. You get a little excited at the opportunities before you.

As you near the sidewalk, a person exits each door and steps out to greet you. They are unaware of each other. As they both begin speaking, you suddenly feel a little unsure about which person you should choose. You stop walking and pause in the gutter.

The 'advisor' is saying words like "stock market, stocks, bonds, risk, returns, portfolio, and allocation." Your head swirls.

The 'insurance agent' talks about how to help protect you, your estate, your family, and your loved ones. You hear words like "guaranteed returns, less risk, annuity, and insurance." Your head swims even more.

They start talking to each other, about you.

"I can earn you 7% per year."

"I can guarantee that you and your family are protected."

"I can grow your money."

"I can mitigate your risk through diversification."

"I can get you tax-free benefits."

"I can help you retire at sixty-five."

"I can insure you and help you grow your wealth."

Suddenly, their faces exude anger. They begin to blame each other.

"You don't do this."

"You don't do that."

"Don't listen to him."

"You want to listen to me."

They continue to argue among themselves.

What do you do? Do you go with the 'advisor' or the 'insurance agent'? Or do you walk away and do nothing? It feels like a tough choice, right?

As if that's not hard enough, the financial industry is confusing in and of itself. Financial language is baffling. Financial options are perplexing. The stock market and banking choices add to the confusion. Knowing who to turn to for support is…well, stressful. All this uncertainty may lead you to feel apathetic about your finances.

When you hand your responsibilities to someone else, you create an expectation that they must deliver. Financial professionals do their best to manage your finances for you; however, the uncertainty in the market may let you down. Problems arise when you are not able to vocalize your desires, and you go with what the financial professionals tell you. When you pass the buck, you take zero ownership of the outcome. You may not invest in what feels right. You may simply look for easy money. You want wealth without the responsibility. But remember, the responsibility is always yours.

Can you handle that responsibility?

You cannot have wealth while effectively running from responsibility. It will catch up to you. It will find you and make you choose.

This is where a secondary issue comes into play. You need to be in alignment with *you*. What do *you* need? What are *your* wants? What are *your* values?

This is another area where I have had clients struggle. They wanted the responsibility, but they weren't in alignment with what *they* wanted and who *they* were. They were seeking success according to what *others* told them they should want. Whether it was their parents, spouses, children, or financial advisors, they were living according to someone else's dreams. They were out of alignment from their own truth, desires, and gifts. When I began to realize this in them, I also saw it inside of me.

I, too, was not living according to what felt correct for me. I was going through the motions of doing what society told me was right. Go to school. Get a job. Work hard. Keep going even when you want to stop. I may not have always known who I am, but the breadcrumbs were always there for me to follow.

It was through one such breadcrumb that I discovered the Human Design System. This is a tool I use with every client with whom I work. A tool that illuminates your individual energetic blueprint design so you can align with *your* inner magnificence and wealth potential. Human Design was the catalyst to me seeing that my greatest potential was locked within me, and I had the key.

I was flooded with realizations of where I was not living true to myself. Where I was pushing harder than I should. I was working in an unsustainable way. For everything I had done right in my work life, I felt like I was falling down and burning out. Then I was beating myself up for it when, all along, I was fighting myself and my truth. I began to see that so much of myself was influenced by others, including my financial beliefs. They had come from outside of me. They were not mine.

Even my fears were not really mine. Like the fear that I may not fit in the financial world as an expert, because my love of numbers was awkward and different. Or the fear that I wouldn't succeed because I was motivated by serving, not by money. I even held the financial fear that if I didn't save and hoard, I would not have enough for the future.

It was through these realizations that I saw that my love of numbers comes from within me. No one else told me it was there. I just knew. Just like no one has to tell me of my love for financial responsibility or my gift and passion for serving. I can feel it; it is who I am. What I am innately and naturally good at is part of my passion. It is a part of my purpose. It comes easily, and it's fun.

So, I shifted my focus and the way in which I worked, because it didn't suit the person I had become. It also didn't serve my clients. I couldn't be my highest and best self if I was letting other people's fears define me and hold me back from my true potential. It was time to let go of those old lies and create new truths for myself. I realized that I loved my work with numbers…and the meaning they create in our lives. I also found that I had a gifted ability to see beyond the numbers. To see inside my clients.

I am an expert here to show you the possibilities *you* can create. I am here to lead you, teach you, and guide you to see your powerful talents and make the decisions that are correct for *you*. I guide you to understand your relationship with money. It lights me up with excitement when I dive into *your* beliefs, emotions, and fears around money. It fulfills me to guide you to manage your money by creating the strategies that allow *you* to invest, save, earn, spend, and donate in ways that make you feel comfortable. Where you take on your own financial responsibility with joy and purpose in order to create your own level of freedom.

This is not the norm. In fact, most people have been taught to find a financial professional, give up their financial responsibility, and hope that their money will grow. That, as if by magic, their money will accumulate and grow, easily and exponentially. That the advisor can mitigate the risks so they can sit back and reap the rewards—with little effort or value creation.

I want you to recognize that you get to choose with whom you work. It is a two-way street. If you have a financial professional who tells you what to do because they are the expert that knows best; who doesn't want to listen to your needs, they may not be the professional for you. If you've heard of a new financial option and your advisor doesn't want to have a conversation about it, get curious. Ask them why, and then see how you feel about their response. Does it resonate? Does it feel untrue for you? At that point, you get to decide what feels correct for you, even if it means finding a new financial person.

When seeking a financial professional, have patience as you perform your due diligence and interview to find that right professional who will serve you and your needs. Ask them about their personal beliefs. Ask them about their financial experiences—both good and bad. Make sure they are a fiduciary, someone who puts *your* best interest first, above their own. Seek the person who is open to discussing various options and possibilities with you. Trust that you will find the support you need.

A good financial planner will create a financial wellness team designed to support you in achieving your desired financial well-being. This team may consist of a CFP®, a CPA, an estate planning attorney, an insurance agent, a financial therapist, and/or a family therapist.

You want all these professionals working together, fighting for you and your financial future. You want them to listen to you and your biggest dreams and goals. You do not want them fighting against you, telling you what to do, or ignoring your needs. Yes, you need someone who has the expertise, but you also need someone who is willing to learn about what you need and want. A financial professional who guides you to discover your truth, your passion, and your path to financial well-being.

Here's the thing, you may not know where you want to go or how to get there, but when options are presented to you about your financial future, you will get a feeling, as to whether or not it feels right for you. If there is any hesitation or procrastination, it is because you are either not ready, there is some resistance, or you may be out of alignment with the option offered. Trust yourself and your truth. Choose the professional that allows you to trust the intuition you possess.

You are invited to realize that your truth is within you. You already know exactly what you want. You already know exactly what feels right for you. You just need the right kind of guidance to get you in alignment with your truth, so you can *be*.

It's no longer about what you *do* in order to *have* so you can *be* in the world. No. It is all about you *being* so you can *do* your work and *have* all that you desire. Your financial well-being starts within you. Your *being* then leads to your purpose and path.

As you peel back the layers of yourself to discover more of who you are, you may be as surprised as I was to learn about the beautiful gifts hidden away. You may notice your beliefs start to shift. If you once thought that you were not good with money, you may now choose to say that every day you are getting *better* with managing your money.

It's time you are guided to honor your gifts, your loves, and your passions. When you align with the truth of who you are—prosperity, wealth, abundance—they become a natural occurrence in your life. You create from that inner power to reflect externally the value you add to the world. When you then take responsibility for all your value creation, there is pride only *you* can express. No financial advisor can do that for you.

I take a bold stand for you to listen to your truth and align with who you are, so you can take control of your financial well-being.

I want you to see the magnificent wealth potential that is right there inside of you, ready to be unleashed. I know that when you live in alignment, you create more value in the world. I want you to share your value in a way that allows you to thrive personally, professionally, and financially. I want you to prosper and have all that you desire.

I want you to realize that *you* are your greatest and most valuable asset. The more you invest in *you*, the more you focus on growing your mental capital, your relational capital, and your well-being capital. All of that is worth so much more than a dollar value.

I want all of this for you because this is what I have realized for myself. Through the confusion, the lack of trusting myself, and diminishing my own love for numbers, I realized that I am enough. I can have it all. The prosperity that I desire is already right here…within me.

I recognize the changes I have made. I am grateful for where I am now and for where I have been along my journey. Each day is a new day for blessings to come through new challenges. I am grateful to have realized my love of numbers. I am excited to share that love with you so you too can find a spark of joy and fun in taking control of your financial well-being. When you are on track with who you really are, you naturally incorporate your financial well-being into all parts of your life.

I want all of that for you. I want that for all of us.

Lessons Learned:

1) *You* are your greatest asset. Invest in yourself every chance you get.

2) Your truth is always within you. Discover who you are, and your truth will be set free.

3) Recognize the innate value you add to the world. The more value you express out into the world, the more it comes back to you. You are the creator of value.

Mindset Tips:

1) No matter what someone else says to you, remember that *you* are good enough.

2) When you deeply and completely love and accept yourself, you are in the flow of abundance. All that you desire finds you.

3) Support is always there, you simply need to ask for it. To learn more about who you really are, request your free Human Design chart at www.ProsperityAlignment.com/how.

Aha Moments and Self Reflections

Note your Thoughts

Donna Eriksson

Innovative mentor, Donna Eriksson has been a driving force in the local beauty industry for over thirty years. Beloved by her clients, valued by her students, and respected by her peers, this premiere aesthetician stands for excellence, integrity and superlative customer service.

However, her success didn't happen overnight. Donna's road was long, with few opportunities to seek guidance, particularly in the practical side of running a business. Thus, her latest venture, to provide both technical training as well as business skills and strategies came into being.

Recognizing the need for 'creative by nature' salon owners to take advantage of training in how to attract clients, Donna now provides mentorship they can use to maximize their success. Their progress has become her passion.

As Donna succinctly puts it, "I teach the 'Beauty of Business' to people in the 'Business of Beauty'," although certainly her expert insights are valuable to any business owner in any field.

Connect with Donna:

donna@ravenesthetics.com

Chapter 2

Are Your Beliefs Yours or Someone Else's?

By Donna Eriksson

*"Money is not everything, but it ranks right up there with
oxygen, and when you need it, you really need it."*
- Zig Ziglar

We come into this world and learn from those that influence us.
What they believe, we believe. You might remember laughing as
a child just because your parents were laughing—even if you
didn't get the joke. The same principle applies to money whether
good or bad, helpful or hurtful, those beliefs become ours too.

As we grow, we are exposed to different beliefs, different ways of
being. Maybe we change from the ideas we grew up with. But
what most of us never give any consideration to is our core beliefs
around money. You may have even grown up hearing things like,
"Money doesn't grow on trees," or, "Only the rich get richer," and
even "Nothing ever comes to us in the middle class."

Think back to your family when you were growing up. Name the
money mantra that was echoed in your home. Whatever it was,
chances are you still believe it now. But the truth is it's not yours.
You took on that mantra because you had no way of knowing any
other way to be. But here's the thing—you can redefine what
money means to you now at this point in your life.

To move forward in life with the kind of relationship with money
that will bring you what you desire, you must first determine for
yourself what you hold true about money.

Let go of any money blocking beliefs that keep you stuck. God wants you to have everything you desire, so stop blocking yourself with belief systems that aren't yours.

"My girl, you can do anything you want."

I heard this from my mom throughout my life. She was undoubtedly my number one cheerleader. It's curious to me how we can hear something all our lives and not be impacted by those words until we stop hearing them. You see, it's only since Mom died that I have *really* reflected on who I am.

In the movie *Forrest Gump*, Forrest says, "Funny how you remember some things and some things you can't. I don't remember being born; I don't recall what I got for my first Christmas or when I went on my first outdoor picnic. But I do remember the first time I heard the sweetest voice in the wide world."

I believe memory has a lot to do with emotion. Not just any emotion, though, a true, strong emotion. I don't have any memories until the age of five when my little brother was born.

At that age, I had no opinion of money or what it meant in my life. To me, we always seemed to be pretty much like everyone else we knew. We were the same, for the most part, as the rest of the family and the same as the other kids at school.

It wasn't until my teen years that I started becoming more aware of the goings on with my family. At this point, my parents were divorced, and I lived with my mom. She worked full-time all my life because I believe she truly liked working *and* because she needed to. As a one income home, Mom, at times, worked both a full and part-time job. This meant I helped a lot with my little brother. It was through these years that I heard phrases such as, "Money's hard to come by," "The rich get richer," and "You can't win for losing." I knew it meant we didn't always get those things that we saw the other kids getting. For us, a summer holiday involved visiting our dad or grandparents. It definitely wasn't visiting places like Disneyland or Mexico like some of the other people around us were doing.

I was hearing opposing information. On the one hand I would hear, "I could do anything I wanted," but on the other hand I'd hear that "money is hard to come by." Despite these conflicting messages, I am grateful that the positive mantra stood out for me and stuck with me throughout my life. You see, because of my biggest cheerleader, Mom, I bought my first business at the age of twenty-one. It never crossed my mind *not* to buy it. Had I run a business before? No. Was I an accountant? Absolutely not. I was an esthetician that most definitely thought I could whatever I wanted to in life.

This was pure craziness coming from a kid who grew up with a parent who lived paycheck to paycheck. Here's the thing, though—I love learning. I learned how to keep the books from month-to-month. I learned from my now husband, then boyfriend, how to budget. We had also bought our first home together within three years because we could. We created a budget that enabled us to have the money we needed. I was on a high and loving life.

I was twenty-four years old, had my own business, and owned (well, along with the bank) my own home with a wonderful man. My mom, to my knowledge, only ever owned a home once in her life. Living paycheck to paycheck meant we had to move every six months. I thought it was normal, so to have a home that I lived in for much longer than six months (we spent nine years in house number one) was delightful.

Now, you're probably thinking I must have had a nice income coming in from my business. Are you ready for the truth? At that point, the only thing the previous owner of my salon had taught me about running the business was the monthly books. I wasn't taught about income statements or creating spreadsheets to compare and track progress year over year. When the accountant would tell me at year-end that we made money and would pay taxes, I would think to myself, *How the hell did that happen because the bank account right now sure doesn't reflect that statement.*

I watched my mom be responsible every month and pay her bills, sometimes (hell, probably most times) leaving very little for us at the end. So, I did the same with my business. (Watching our family is where we learn most of our lessons.) Everything else got paid first. The staff, rent, suppliers, government (look out if you don't pay them) and whatever else came up got paid first.

And something else *always* came up.

Then I took whatever was left. For years, I paid myself about $500 a month. I, of course, worked the most in my business and took home the least. I didn't know any other way because no one had ever taught me any differently.

After thirteen years at my salon, I was offered a full-time position with a local beauty salon supplier. I had been working with them for a few years already on a contractor basis. Now that I had a little one, I took the position, wanting to be home more (yes, working for someone else meant I would be home more, which was good news to my ears).

So, what did I do with the salon?

I walked away. I was tired and wanted it to be done. I signed it over to a beautiful young woman I had been working with for several years. To keep the business would have meant a lot of work doing the bookkeeping, ordering, staffing, and maintenance. I was truly done. The fork was stuck in me, and I was truly thoroughly cooked.

Looking back, it's the only thing in my life I regret. However, I wholeheartedly believe it to be a part of my soul's journey; a lesson I was meant to learn.

Fast forward another thirteen years (that number seems to signal change for me). I left the beauty salon supplier (in the full-time capacity at least, because I still worked on a contractor basis). I started another business, but this time on a smaller scale. The business was run out of my house. I used my own money, small increments at a time, and started doing what I do. You see, I had always kept a handful of esthetic clients through the years anyway, so now all I had to do was to go out there and get some more.

The best thing I did to get this business off the ground (and essential with no storefront) was to go out to networking events and become involved with my local Chamber of Commerce. I was on the board for the Chamber for a couple of years, which got me in front of a lot of new people. I also worked local markets and events that I felt were a good fit for me at the time.

Today, I am seven years into this business, and I'm grateful to say I've come a long way, baby.

I worked with a business coach for four years to learn the skills and strategies to help me to work on building my business up. Those skills that no one had ever taught me before. I invested in myself and followed my intuition because I felt like it had done a good job at self-directed learning earlier in my life. Lifelong learning—it's my passion. And it's what I love sharing with those that are ready to learn.

I also learned that *no one* can build their business alone. You need support. You need to learn from someone who has gone before you and learned the hard lessons already. There's no need to reinvent the wheel.

So, at this stage in my journey, I can honestly say that I love, love, *love* the balance I have in life. I get to work as much as I want, which allows me to make time for my family when they need me.

Most importantly: I pay *myself* first. I have learned to watch and understand my numbers: the income statement, profit and loss statement, balance sheet, and I know about measuring profitability. Making money is the easy part. Knowing how to manage it is what takes learning. That's okay, though, it's the same for all of us, and it's important to remember that it's okay to ask for help when you need support.

When you've sought help, you need to practice, practice, practice what you've just been taught. No one gets good at anything from doing it only once or twice. You've heard the saying, "Your thoughts become your words, your words become your behavior, your behaviors become your habits, your habits become your values, and your values become your destiny." It couldn't be more truthful.

After more than three decades in my industry and more than two decades owning my own businesses, here's what I know: long-term success with money (both personal and professional) comes down to consistency with your daily habits, repetition, and a willingness to be open to learning new skills.

Like a space shuttle making my way through this journey—each section being released and activated at the right time. I truly believe the next part of my journey has just begun.

Lessons Learned:

1) Do what you say you're going to do. If you can't or don't want to do something, say no. It's key to your integrity.

2) Know your numbers. Look at your finances, if not daily, then at least weekly. Knowing where you stand gives you choice.

3) Do whatever it takes. When you set yourself a goal, you have the power within you to bring it to fruition. Do the work.

Mindset Tips:

1) Consistency and persistence will move you toward your goals.

2) Don't make a permanent decision based on your temporary emotion.

3) Good daily habits yield results. Set yourself a daily routine that increases your productivity.

Aha Moments and Self Reflections

Note your Thoughts

Tiffany Keeping

Tiffany Keeping is a financial broker, yoga instructor, and aspiring author in Edmonton, Alberta whose mission is to help people create wealth and security. She is especially passionate about helping women create financial success and start living the lives of their dreams.

After experiencing a major financial setback from the Fort McMurray fire, Tiffany decided to commit her life to ensuring that others received the financial education and tools necessary to live a life of financial stability and security, with the goal of working towards financial freedom. She finds joy in educating others about living a financially successful life by teaching them the rules of the money game.

As a licensed financial educator, she works with women, men, and families to create and build prosperity so they can live the life of their dreams.

Connect with Tiffany:

keepingtiffany@gmail.com

Chapter 3

Beauty Come Out of the Beast

By Tiffany Keeping

On May 3, 2016, as I watched the fire blazing in my rear view mirror while I was driving down Highway 63 alone with my babies and my pets, I knew my life was about to change. At that moment, I had no idea to what degree my life would change…a new home, a new career, and a new life plan.

The Beast forced me to really internalize that I was not fully immersed and involved in my family's finances because we weren't as financially prepared as we needed to be. Most readers will not have to go through the same kind of life change that I did by having to escape a city while watching it burn in your rear view mirror. However, I feel that most readers will at some point go through a financial challenge in their life and relationship. It was not until tragedy struck my family that I started really opening up to my partner about our finances, financial achievements, financial failures, and my personal financial aspirations. Isn't it funny how when we lose everything that we finally start being fully transparent about all our hopes, dreams and wishes?

My hope and intention while writing this chapter is that by sharing my story it will inspire you to become more involved in your financial life and your financial aspirations. Financial independence is available for everyone and with good support and planning it can be achieved.

Couples and Money

We each bring our own money stories into the relationship, but do most of us sit down and talk to our partner about money and our beliefs surrounding money? Also, how do the money beliefs, stories, and mindsets that our parents instilled in us, impact our money choices and personal stories as adults and subsequently as couples?

Being married for almost fifteen years, I realized that I haven't had much of a deep discussion about my money stories with my partner nor heard his beliefs regarding money. Considering the statistics about money and divorce, it seems rather odd that I wouldn't have already had a detailed conversation with my spouse about our finances. It seems like this should be a standard conversation that most couples have before they become a couple; especially before they choose to live together and definitely before they get married. Also, I believe it's important for couples to discuss what their parents' money beliefs, stories, and mindsets were and how those translated into each of their individual beliefs. I think it is important to remember that you may not be aware of how your parents' beliefs impact your decisions around money. Often, many couples have opposing money beliefs, and therefore your parents might have very different mindsets about how to handle their finances. It might be hard for you to recognize which parent you take after. So, I recommend talking to your partner or spouse about how they view your money mindset as it might give your deeper insight into your beliefs.

Looking back at my financial decisions throughout my adult life, I have to question how much influence my parents and their beliefs impacted my money decisions, beliefs, and mindset. I grew up in a divorced family with my mom as my primary caregiver as many children did in the 80s and 90s. I visited my father every other weekend, and he remarried when I was about eleven. Since

I grew up in a blended family, I technically had three parents that could influence my money mindset. My husband, however, grew up in a nuclear family giving him less of a pool of influence. I'm not sure if these differences had a significant impact on our money mindsets, but I feel strongly that it might have. I tend to lean more towards my mother's money mindsets, decisions, influences, and beliefs, which make me more apt to prepare for worst-case scenarios rather than have more of an abundance mindset. My mother was the type of woman who budgeted, saved and prepared for retirement and financial emergencies. My mom always talked to myself and my sister about the importance of good insurance coverage, saving for retirement and ensuring we had an emergency fund. I feel that because she put so much emphasis on these aspects of financial planning and security that it added extra strain on my marriage because my husband did not hold the same values.

"According to the poll by the Bank of Montreal (TSX:BMO), 68% of those surveyed say fighting over money would be their top reason for divorce, followed by infidelity (60%) and disagreements about family (36%)."[1] I find it interesting that couples today find money more of a contentious issue and a reason for divorce than infidelity. I'm sure these statistics would surprise a lot of people. However, I think it shows that individuals want to live a financially successful life and they are not necessarily willing to have their future negatively influenced or impacted by their partner's decisions.

Every relationship has financial trials, tribulations, successes and total friggin' wins. In my relationship, it always seemed so much more tranquil when we were riding a success or win than when we were riding a downward spiral. Unfortunately, we

---

[1] https://business.financialpost.com/personal-finance/couples-more-willing-to-forgive-spouse-for-cheating-than-money-problems-bmo-survey-finds

experienced one of the bigger financial, emotional and spiritual setbacks that any family can survive; one that we are still working on making a complete comeback from. In doing so, it will make our family stronger and help us grow into more loving and giving people.

Throughout our relationship, my partner and I, like most couples, have had many ups and downs with our finances from paying for university, funding a wedding, buying our first home, selling said home and subsequently purchasing several other homes during our marriage. Some of these ventures have had great financial returns while others have created great losses. Some of these ventures have been discussed thoroughly with each other while others were decisions we made individually. Of course, most of the financially detrimental decisions that have been made were ones that each of us made on our own without direction or discussion with the other partner.

Our most devastating loss happened with one such decision. This type of decision and delegation, I would wager, happens in most relationships, partnerships or marriages since many of us take on certain roles and responsibilities within our relationship, whether we do it consciously or subconsciously. There are some very obvious roles, and responsibilities that come to your mind when you think of a married couple such as the husband will tend to fix things around the home while the wife tends to do more of the cleaning and cooking. Obviously, these standard roles are not 100% true all the time. I'm using these roles as examples to paint a picture of the typical gender roles that exist and how these roles carry over into our financial decision making, authority, and power within a relationship. For example, most women tend to be more involved in the day-to-day spending and budgeting while men tend to be more involved in managing the family investments. As I have said previously, these typical gender roles are not true 100% of the time and nor should they be expectations of the role that you must take in your own relationship.

I hope that by telling you my story, you will choose to be more involved and maybe challenge the typical roles that we allow ourselves to slide into during a relationship. It's easy to slip into the roles and responsibilities that we find easy, but that doesn't mean they are the right role for us and it also doesn't mean that we have absolute control over the duties within that role. It is so important that your partner understands the roles and responsibilities you undertake within your financial home and that your partner understands how to take on those responsibilities in the event you are unable to perform them for any reason. If you are the one who does the online banking and bill paying then make sure your partner is set up to log into your account and that you train them on how to pay the bills so they could assume this role in your absence, if need be.

When my family moved up to Fort McMurray the previous May in 2015, my husband fulfilled his typical financial duty, which was to call the insurance company and put insurance on our home that we had rented. He had done this very same thing for every home we purchased and every place we rented during our whole entire relationship, so I didn't think anything of it, and I didn't ask any questions about our rental insurance on this property. When the policy came in the mail the very next week, I filed it in our insurance file in our filing cabinet without looking at its contents or ensuring that we were properly covered. I assumed that we were covered for the same amount we had always been covered for and that nothing had changed. This was a major mistake on my part, and I didn't find out how big a mistake until after the fire.

A very important lesson can be learned here: don't ever assume. Don't ever assume that things will always remain the same. Don't ever assume that someone will do things the same way they have always done things. Don't ever assume that your partner knows or understands what needs to be done. You can pass a responsibility onto your partner, which they may accept, but that doesn't mean that they know how to execute said responsibility and it will definitely not be done that way you would do it or the way you want it to be done.

I assumed that my husband had done what he had always done and he never told me that he made any changes and I didn't ask. I chose to assume that everything was the same. I now understand that this was a life lesson for me. One where I learned not to blame another person for 100% of the situation when things went wrong. I assure you it took me a number of years after the fire to come to the conclusion that I was partially responsible for the mess we created.

There is never a situation be it financial, emotional, spiritual or physical that you are not partially responsible for putting yourself in. It's easy for us to blame others and say, "Well it's their fault that we have credit card debt," or "it's their fault that we didn't get that house," or it's their fault that we lost money on that investment." Whatever that blame scenario; it's never 100% the other person's fault. You had a hand in the outcome as well. That is also not to say that the responsibility or fault is 50/50 either. 50/50 responsibility is a rare occurrence but just because it wasn't 50% your doing doesn't mean you aren't responsible for some aspect of the situation you find yourself in today.

I chose not to ask questions or look at our new insurance policy. If you asked me today, I wish I had done one of those things because I would have found out that my wonderful husband had decided to cut our content insurance in half, which left us underinsured by half. Now here is another important lesson: just because your partner takes on a financial role within your financial home doesn't mean they know what they are doing. I had bestowed my husband with the task of setting up our insurance policy, but I didn't take into account that he hadn't the foggiest idea how much the stuff in our house actually cost and therefore he had no idea that he had underinsured us until it was too late. Had I been involved in the set up of this rental insurance policy none of this would have happened. I had a really good idea of what the items in our home cost to repurchase or replace. I should know as I bought most of the items. So, why did I put him in charge of a task that was clearly more suited for myself? I don't know. I guess because we had always done it that way and that is the worst reason to continue to do anything.

Should my husband have talked to me about the changes he made? Absolutely. Should he have consulted me before making any changes? Yes, I believe so. Should he have told me about the changes he decided to make? Absolutely. Did this make it easy for me to blame him when our home burned to the ground in the Fort McMurray fire? Oh, it most definitely did.

But, here's the funny thing about blame, it usually includes a healthy dose of hurt and anger that fuels the finger-pointing. And the even more hilarious thing is that the anger you feel isn't usually directed at the other person; most often it is directed at yourself. Because deep down you know that you had a hand in the situation that you find yourself in. I was angry at myself for not asking a question and for not looking at the insurance policy to make sure it covered us for the right amount. I was angry at myself for being so disconnected with our finances. I was angry and hurt that I trusted my husband with this important task and I felt that he failed me and that he failed our family. Looking back, I don't think it was fair of me to put those expectations on my husband that he was clearly not able to fulfill.

I was hurt and angry for a very long time. I was upset that my husband would make such an impactful decision without consulting me first. I was even more upset that he didn't feel the need to tell me at all that he had made this type of drastic change to our coverage. I was mostly upset that I had to find out from the insurance company after the fire that he had lowered our coverage because my husband had forgotten that he had even made this important decision in the first place. Needless to say, the moment I found out that our coverage had been lowered to half the amount that we needed, I threatened to file for divorce. I was so upset with the whole mess. I felt betrayed, deceived, and more importantly, lied to by the one person who had sworn to love me till death do us part. Now, this could've been the end of the story. I could have filed for divorce and tried to move on. However, I decided to stay and figure out what went wrong and tried and fix the situation. I wasn't ready to give up just yet even though I was beyond livid.

Now, there will be people reading this story who would think I would be justified in walking away. I'm sure there are even more people who think I should have walked away after not being consulted or told of this change and more importantly that my husband didn't ever tell me of his decision to change our coverage. The insurance company told us when I finally pressed my husband to find out how much they were covering. It would have been easy to blame him for everything and walk away, but I didn't want to be one of those statistics. I had married my best friend, and I wasn't willing to quit on him just yet. It takes a lot of courage to try and make things work and fix whatever mess is created. It sometimes comes with harsh judgment from friends, family, and society. I feel like financial betrayal is akin to infidelity. The trust has been broken, and you feel deceived and betrayed by your partner. It's not an easy thing to move past or work through. There are still moments that I slide back into old patterns and delegate tasks to my husband as does he, but we will try to work more as a team now and communicate more with each other.

The number one thing that went wrong in our relationship was is a breakdown in communication. This can happen to a lot of couples. You get so comfortable with each other that you think you know what the other person wants, so you don't bother to ask their opinion. The most important thing you can do in your relationship is ask your partner what they think and how they feel about money, their dreams or just life in general. Your relationship with your money is a reflection of your relationship with yourself. Therefore, your joint financial relationship with money is a reflection of your relationship with each other. So, you must ask yourself, does your financial situation reflect the type of relationship you want with each other? If the answer is yes, keep doing what you're doing. If not, now is the time to make a change in a positive direction. Set a financial date with your partner and discuss the hits and misses in your financial home and take the necessary steps to fix the misses. If you are not sure where to begin then consider speaking with a reputable financial professional who helps clients with financial planning, goal setting, debt management, and budgeting.

The lack of communication in our relationship cost us money. I hope to impart my wisdom on you and implore you to take a more active role in all the aspects of your finances. No one expects you to be perfect at budgeting or rock your investments like a financial broker, but this is where finding a good professional can help make your financial vision a reality. Needless to say, after the fire took our house and we had to face the challenges of rebuilding our life with less money than we needed to do so I definitely took a more active role in our finances. My husband and I definitely talked more about our finances and our goals for the future. We have now instituted a money date night so that we are both on the same page. We also started talking about how our parents influenced our money habits. As I tend to be a saver and my husband is more of a spender it has caused a lot of arguments and tension. It has been very helpful putting those stories to words and verbalizing our feelings as it helps us understand the other person's perspective.

Now, I know there are going to be more trials and tribulations in the future. I don't know if there will be another situation where I will feel betrayed, deceived or lied to by my partner. There is never a guarantee issued along with your marriage certificate, but I know that if you try to always work through a situation from a loving perspective then whatever the outcome it will be of the highest good for you. So, say it with me everyone: *love*. I will treat my money with *love*. I will treat my finances with *love*. I will love myself enough to be present and active in my financial home. I will treat my partner with love. I will communicate with *love*.

Lessons Learned:

1) Never play the blame game. No matter what the situation both parties are responsible for the success or failure of your money situation. *Communicate, Communicate, Communicate.* You'll avoid trouble if you sit down and talk honestly about your finances.

2) Try out all of the financial roles within your household. You might be surprised which responsibilities you like and which ones you are great at, but also make sure you include your partner in your decisions and duties.

3) Ask a financial professional help to make sure you are on track and working towards the life you want to live. Just like hiring any other professional, make sure you vet this person thoroughly and always hire someone you can trust. Never forget, a good professional wants you to succeed.

Mindset Tips:

1) Remember, money has an energy and frequency, it will be attracted to you based on your energetic frequency. As a couple it is important to try to both be working on your same frequency so you can attract the money, assets and people you want into your life.

2) Every three to six months, set up a 'financial date' with your partner, where you check in with each other and discuss how the journey is going and if it's getting you toward your dreams. Focusing on your dreams will help you both create your dream life so don't forget to dream big together.

3) And of course, I leave the most important tip for last, always remember *people* matter, money *doesn't*. *People* matter, *stuff* doesn't. Speak from a place of love instead of fear as this will help put you both in a successful mindset where you can create the life of your dreams.

Aha Moments and Self Reflections

Note your Thoughts

Amanda Kendall

Amanda Kendall has been an entrepreneur for over fifteen years. She has an extensive background in tax and accounting, where she has spent the majority of her career helping entrepreneurs work through tax concerns that were caused by financial difficulties. After experiencing her own financial difficulty in her business and discovering the root cause of it, she started working with entrepreneurs to prevent financial difficulty in their businesses.

Through her business, Elevating Profits, LLC Amanda puts an emphasis on engineering profits and paying yourself what you are worth. This, in turn, creates a viable business that can sustain minor financial difficulties and can predict and avoid major ones.

Connect with Amanda:

Amanda@elevatingprofits.com

Chapter 4

Profit is Your Responsibility

By Amanda Kendall

It had been ten long months…the most challenging, grueling, emotional ten months I had ever endured in my entire life. My marriage and business were on the verge of collapsing. I had not taken a paycheck from my business in ten months, so I was almost broke. I was behind on my mortgage, worried my utilities would be shut off and afraid I would go to the grocery store to buy food for my kids, and my card would be declined because, in my attempt to keep up appearances, I was writing checks to pay bills with money that was not in the account at the time the check was signed.

I was an emotional wreck on the inside, but on the outside, no one suspected a thing. I disguised it all so well that some days, I could almost convince myself that things were not that bad.

On the outside, I was this successful businesswoman who had everything. I had a great marriage, a happy and beautiful family, and a business that was flourishing. And by all definitions of revenue, my business *was* flourishing. I was grossing over $600,000 in revenue annually in my small business. I had seven employees plus myself at the peak of my downward spiral. To the outsider looking in, how could that not equal success?

But on the inside, my business was in debt to the tune of $150,000.00 from loans I had taken out to keep things running that year. The loans were not your typical bank loans—these were high interest, weekly payment loans. I was putting out almost $12,000 a month in loan repayments alone. The result of this was paying off one loan as fast as I could so I could pull out another one to cover the other loan payments. I was borrowing from Peter to pay Paul and then borrowing from Paul to repay Peter again. The cycle was terrifying.

Payroll was always a scary situation. I had to stop taking a paycheck to make sure I could pay all the employees and pay the taxes. If I took a paycheck, then taxes would not get paid, and that was a slippery slope I was not even going to potentially start sliding down.

Looking back, nothing that happened should have been a surprise. I could have seen it all coming had my attention been in the right places. I had some outside distractions that had pulled my focus away from the business without me even realizing it at the time. As the saying goes, it wasn't personal; it was business.

But let me tell you, when it *is* personal, it can impact your business without you even realizing it is happening. You will find yourself at a point of not taking a paycheck for months on end and facing every backup and security blanket you had in effect being ripped away from you.

Let me back up and take you through my story. Letting go of control, knowingly or unknowingly, seemed to be a repeating theme throughout my journey. There were times where I threw my hands up and gave in to the pressure so that I could concentrate on where I thought *all* my focus needed to be. There were times where I simply had no control over what was going on in my business. It didn't matter that my skewed view at the time was that I was in complete control of everything.

My business took a lot of my time and attention away from what really mattered. My husband had resented me for that, and in turn, he resented my business, even though it helped to pay the bills. I think we both had an expectation that after the first year or so of the business being opened, I would not have to work so hard, that things would get easier, and the money would provide for our family. If you are an entrepreneur, you know this is not how business works for most people, and I was one of them.

I found myself working even harder than I had when I had worked for someone else. The long hours and late nights took a toll on family and my health. The money paid the bills in the beginning, but that was about it. There was not a lot of extra and, most months, it still felt like things were paycheck to paycheck in our household.

In an effort to save my marriage, I did things in the business and made decisions that I would not have normally made. I wanted more. I felt like if I could produce more revenue in the business that I could relieve some of the money stress by being able to take a larger paycheck. My solution to making more money was to hire sales staff. Now, I am a believer that if you put something out in the universe that the solution will eventually come. No sooner did I decide I wanted to bring in a dedicated sales staff did I receive an email from a gentleman who worked in sales in my industry asking to meet to discuss a position with my firm.

I met with him and decided to hire him, even though I knew he was going to require a higher salary than I was immediately comfortable paying him. But I also knew that if I could make it work that it would increase revenue in my business each month, allowing me to produce a greater profit. Thus, the first loan for my business was taken out in order to have enough operating capital to know I could get through the initial start-up phase of the sales department for my small business.

In my ever-present desire for more, I had made a hasty decision without laying out all the expectations of the situation. I ended up hiring more sales staff in an attempt to produce even more revenue for the business. Increased revenue, in my mind, meant increased profits. Bigger profits meant a larger paycheck for me. Isn't this how it all works?

What I hadn't factored in was that in addition to increased revenue, all these steps I was taking to increase business revenues would also increase business expenses and overhead costs.

The first loan I had taken out was a weekly payment, and once we hired more sales staff, the business struggled to cover the increased overhead and payroll costs. It also meant it was harder to make that weekly loan payment. It was at this time that I thought about taking a second loan for the business would help offset the stress I was feeling every time I looked at my bank account.

What I really should have done at this point was sat down and ran my numbers. I needed to know at this point what I had to produce from the sales department for it to be profitable, but I had no clue, and in my crisis state of thought, I hadn't even let it cross my mind.

Two months into this 'growth' phase, I had already taken out two loans totaling over $50,000, increased my staff by three people in the sales department, and was trying to cut my hours in the office down so I could spend more time at home and find some balance. A year after expanding, I had been through six employees in the sales department. I had faced situations that did not align with who I was or what my business was, and completely ignored them all in the name of revenue. I found myself taking advice from people I should not have and doing things in the business that hurt me more than helped me. I second guessed myself a great deal during this time— in business and in life.

I had taken out a total of $200,000 in loans over the course of a year and a half. I could not understand how I could have borrowed that much money, yet my business was constantly cash poor. I stopped taking a regular paycheck to make sure my staff could get paid as well as covering all the overhead costs.

It started with my taking only one check a month instead of two. That quickly turned into only taking one check every couple of months, which quickly turned into not taking a paycheck at all. My income from the business turned into about $1000 a month in owner draws to make sure I could cover the necessities and keep all my personal creditors at bay. I paid them every two to three months in order to avoid collections and shut offs.

My mortgage became almost three full months in arrears. My electric bill was getting paid once a quarter. My phone was on the verge of getting cut off every single month. I was feeding my family cheap meals that I could stretch my dollar on. My credit cards were all maxed out regularly with the minimum payment not being made each month.

I had created a cycle in my business and my life that was unsustainable. I thought if I could focus more during my limited hours in the office that I could help produce more revenue alongside the sales department and I could offset the monetary pain I felt whenever I had to run payroll or pay rent.

Office hours were spent behind closed doors, focusing on getting the job done. My time at home was spent only half present with my family while I was thinking of what I could get done after everyone was in bed. I would be up until two or three o'clock in the morning working. I was sleeping an average of two hours per night. Lunch breaks consisted of eating fast food while sitting at my desk while I continued to work. I knew if I worked hard enough and long enough that I could dig myself out of the hole I had ended up in. I didn't lack drive, just the ability to see what was really going on.

This lifestyle I was living ended up taking more of a toll on me than I was willing to acknowledge. It took a mental, physical, and emotional toll on me like nothing else in my life ever had.

My health deteriorated, and I gained almost forty pounds in the span of a little over a year. My doctor was concerned about my cholesterol, and I was depressed to the point of not even wanting to get out of bed most days. I found myself silently crying myself to sleep. I would hide in the bathroom with the shower running while I sat on the bathroom floor and sobbed over the stress of what my life had become. I found myself forgetting simple things like to go grocery shopping or to set alarms to wake-up.

I had become someone I did not recognize.

I then quit paying attention to my business finances. I found it easier to just work and ignore the obvious things that I needed to be dealing with in order to succeed. I felt like I could ignore them out of existence. Rent was always covered, and payroll was always covered. Everything else was simply managed. The hardest part of all of this was I didn't talk to anyone about any of it—not a friend, not a mentor, not even my husband. I held it all in and maintained an image I thought was necessary in the world of business owners. It was my secret to hide, my burden to bear, and I was determined to keep it a secret.

My husband never knew how bad the situation had become. He knew my income had gone down and that I was stressed more than usual about money, but I didn't let him into the inner details of what was going on in the business that were seeping into our personal finances. We had always had separate bank accounts and paid bills separately, so it was pretty easy to hide everything from him.

Twenty-one months after this growth phase had begun and ten long months after my last real paycheck, I hit my breaking point. Enough was enough. I knew it was time to make some big changes.

You know that saying if you want different results, you have to do something different? This moment came for me financially when I hit the tenth month of not taking a paycheck and after taking owner draws of only $10,000. I was facing the worst financial situation I had ever experienced.

Emotionally, this moment came for me when I realized that my business had resulted, in part, in the failure of my marriage. Physically, this point came for me when I weighed more than I had at the time of giving birth to either one of my boys. My doctor said she was officially worried and was considering putting me on medication for not only my cholesterol, but also my depression.

None of this was acceptable to me. I had hit rock bottom, and it was time to pick myself back up and start over, however that looked. I took a little time to reflect on what had gotten me to that point and how I was going to get back on my feet. My reflection, coming from a space of knowing something had to change, allowed me to see things that I had not seen while I was in the thick of everything. I knew I had to turn things around quickly or I would have had to close my business. I was facing being a single mom, which meant not having a steady income was no longer an option. (Going to work for someone else was even less of an option, so I had some motivation there.)

As I reflected and realized that all areas of my life had suffered, I also realized that all areas were connected. When I had let one area of life suffer, it had created a snowball effect into all areas of my life. It was a total loss of control.

I looked at my business and what had gotten me to the breaking point. I took an entire day and locked myself in my office to look at the big picture, but also the little details of the situation. I printed out monthly profit and loss statements, year-end balance sheets, monthly cash flow statements, receivable and payable reports, and payroll summaries all for the previous two years. It was time for me to not only get an idea of *what* had happened but to get an idea of *why*. It was time for me to reestablish the relationship with my business finances that I had had the first three years of my business. I needed to pinpoint where I had allowed things to fall apart—not only for my business but for my sanity as well.

I went month by month, starting with the couple of months prior to opening the sales department. I looked at revenue sources and amounts, expense categories, profit margins, payroll margins to revenues coming in and cash flow in comparison to what was happening. I started mapping out where my loan proceeds had been used and what the return on investment, if any, had been on these loans. (There was not any in case you were wondering.)

I looked at how much revenue the sales department had brought in compared to how much it had cost between payroll and overhead. I analyzed what I had paid per lead for the sales department and how many leads turned into clients. I examined the effective cost of obtaining every client that had come in through my sales department. I looked at these same numbers for myself on the sales I had brought in over the last two years. I did not exempt myself as I needed to know why my business had grown by $150,000 in revenue on average per year, but my losses had been overwhelmingly large.

This whole process took me almost ten hours—ten solid hours with lots of coffee, an energy drink or two, lunch at my desk, and restroom breaks in the middle. I had to break most of these numbers out. I had not separated out payroll in my books by department, nor had I done the best in my clouded judgment over the last couple of years at separating out expenses by department. I had to face some cold, hard facts during those 10 hours that I had buried over the last couple of years.

By the end of the day, I was not happy with the areas I had ignored or let slide that had resulted in part to where I had ended up. Even though I had decided enough was enough, the lack of attention to detail that got me to that point was inexcusable. By the end of the day, though, I had built a solid foundation towards creating the relationship I needed with my numbers in order to have a better financial future for my business.

One of the biggest things I had realized in looking at these numbers was that even though the sales department had increased my revenue by 25% annually, my expenses had increased by almost 36% in conjunction to that increase. Between payroll, overhead, and increased operating expenses for the department, I was spending more money to keep it operating than it had been producing. This was a hard lesson to learn in hindsight. What made it so tough was that had I kept a portion of my attention on the business like it should have been all along, I would have seen the issue very early on and I could have taken corrective actions to either increase the profits from that department or shut it down well before it cost me so much time and money (and more).

One of the first changes I needed to make was to downsize my company. More revenue had not produced more profit, so this was not the answer to being more profitable. This meant that the very next day, I laid off my entire sales department. I eliminated an entire office suite I had been renting and eliminated every expense associated directly with that department. This simple, although large, change over the next month not only allowed for a positive cash flow, but also a draw for $1500 instead of $1000. This alone was a huge step in the right direction for me. All this change made me realize that growth does not correlate to more profit. The profits have to drive the growth, or the growth will sink your business.

I spent some time looking at my sales numbers over not only those horrible two years but also the couple of years prior. I realized that I had let my numbers drop by almost 48% in revenue that I was directly responsible for. This fact contributed to some of the losses in my business, as well. I made a commitment that day to spend a minimum of two hours a day, five days a week on new sales to improve this percentage and get back to where I had been. That commitment, over the course of forty-five days, improved my numbers to the point where I was about 86% of the way back to where my numbers had been prior to my downhill slide.

I also made a commitment that day to spend two hours a week, every single week without exception, with my numbers. If I could not understand where my numbers were then how could I ever expect to make them work the way I needed them to? How could I ever expect to pay myself what I knew I was worth if I wasn't tracking the numbers to know if I could do that?

I had to understand what was profitable for me and what was not. I had to understand the numbers involved with the services I was already offering before I could even consider offering new services. I had to understand where my money was being spent in the business and which of these expenses were necessary. I put a stop to all expenses that were neither necessary nor beneficial. This allowed me in the second month to not only take a draw of $1500 again but also to take one normal paycheck. To say I was ecstatic would be the understatement of my life.

The day I sat down to look over these numbers was right after Thanksgiving. I was looking at a $31,000 loss in my business to date for the year. I closed out that year with a loss of $25,089.73 in my business. This number was not anything to be proud of, but in comparison to where I had been just over thirty days prior, I knew it was a great foundation for where I was heading.

The following year, I honored my commitments and kept up with taking time to review my numbers every week and spending time on new sales every single day. By doing so, I closed out the following year with a profit of $70,000.00. That is a 73% increase in the span of a year. I think it is important to mention here that I did not service many new clients to hit this profit. I added a few new clients to my base, but mostly I started looking at what I was charging and where I was spending. I raised prices to where they needed to be in order to be profitable. I lost a few clients from this but replaced them with new ones that had no issues with my fees. I cut out expenses that were not benefiting the growth, future, or bottom line of my business.

I believe that every entrepreneur can do this same thing in their business. Most of us did not go into business to be an accountant or a bookkeeper, and I am by no means saying you need to spend your valuable time performing these tasks. In fact, outsource these items; it will truly help your bottom line.

However, outsource them to someone whom you can communicate with about your goals and who is willing and able to help you manage what you need to get there. Don't outsource it and forget it, though. It is your duty and obligation if you want to be profitable to know your numbers, to work your numbers, and to understand how they work for you.

There are too many entrepreneurs throwing in the towel and going back to being an employee than should be necessary. If you take the time to work on your business and your business will repay you. Money must be directed in your business, not directing you.

Start small, grow on that, and ask for help when needed. Never step so far out of it that you end up in a situation like I did and have no clue how it happened. If you have a pulse on your business's finances, you will always be able to predict when things are about to happen and be able to fix whatever it is before it gets bad.

Lessons Learned:

1) Your business must be purposely profitable. If profits happen by accident, they will not be around for long without intention.

2) Your business finances must be managed on a regular basis. You have to know your revenues and your costs. Keep a running tally on how your business is doing. This is the only way to ensure profits for the long-term.

3) Revenue does not equal profits. Growing your business just to create more revenue, rarely means more profits. As revenues grow, if you are not intentional, expenses will grow to match, and you find yourself with more work and no growth in profit.

Mindset Tips:

1) Business finance is not math, it is money. With the right guidance and some strategic time, you can learn to love your numbers.

2) Be intentional with your profits. Set them aside intentionally and systematically. By doing so, you prioritize the profits in your business, and they will grow.

3) Sustained profitability has a direct correlation to consistency and your habits. You must be consistent in creating good habits around your business finances.

Aha Moments and Self Reflections

Note your Thoughts

Randy McCord

Randy, an alumnus of the University of Calgary, is a founder of National Best Financial Network, one of the most innovative and progressive life Insurance brokerages in Canada. He is also Exempt Market Licensed and is a private equity specialist with Pinnacle Wealth Brokers.

Randy and his National Best team are protection and investment specialists. However, Randy's personal focus is business clients, whether they are sole proprietors or incorporated businesses. His team is dedicated to assisting business owners who are looking for financial planning expertise.

Randy is a big believer in education. He has facilitated over 500 educational workshops and courses for Canadians in the last twenty years including Investing in Real Estate at Mount Royal University and the Calgary Board of Education in Calgary and Financial Road Map Workshops with his colleagues at National Best.

He has been an ardent investor himself for over thirty-five years and has been licensed in financial services for over twelve years.

Connect with Randy:

randy.mccord@nbbn.ca

Chapter 5

Tax-Free Retirement Income
How to Make it Happen – Legally

By Randy McCord

In the world of financial services, one of the most complex planning problems is retirement; the longer you wait, the more challenging it becomes. Yet, according to a 2016 research survey commissioned by the Ontario Securities Commission, more than 50% of Canadians, fifty years or older, have no retirement plan. The best way to ensure a comfortable retirement is to start early and plan well.

Most financial advisors start the retirement conversation with the end goal in mind. In other words, they will first consider how much retirement income is enough. Once they have that number, it is relatively easy for them to reverse engineer the savings required to reach the goal. The complexity comes with selecting which investment products will produce the desired result given the risk tolerance of the client.

In every case, both parties are looking for a higher rate of return with a lower risk profile.

The advisor will contemplate many factors while setting up an effective retirement plan, such as current and future income, lifestyle, assets, liabilities, inflation and, of course that ever-present pest - taxation. Regardless of their licensing or training, advisors all agree that taxation is a key component of retirement planning. In fact, nearly every financial planning article, commentary, or book, recommends strategies for tax efficiency or preferential taxation of retirement income.

What is rarely discussed in the industry is *tax-free* retirement income. One reason is that the term *tax-free* raises red flags with regulators. They immediately think *tax avoidance*, which is illegal. The truth is that investors and retirees *can* use strategies to mitigate their tax burden if it's permissible under the Tax Act.

Today, we are going to look at two different products that can *legally* generate tax-free retirement income.

The first product, the Tax-Free Savings Account, better known as the TFSA, is relatively new. It was introduced to Canadians in 2009 by the federal government and can be used to create significant tax-free retirement income.

The second product has a very different pedigree and originated in 1762. Can you imagine? A product that has been around for over two hundred and fifty years, cannot be sold by banks, and is rarely mentioned by investment advisors or financial planners? More on that later.

First, I'd like to introduce you to the Case family.

The Cases live in Calgary, have owned their home for five years, and are about to renew their mortgage. The husband, Justin Case, is general manager at a construction company. His wife, Jewel Case, is a dental assistant. They are both thirty-nine years old. They enjoy a comfortable lifestyle and have two children (son, Crank Case, age nine and daughter, Pillow Case, age seven).

Their financial planning has focused mainly on paying off their home, saving in RESP's for their children's education, paying off their vehicles, and saving for their annual vacation.

So far, they have not addressed saving for retirement but, at their monthly family meeting, Jewel mentions a new term she came across while surfing the web: the FIN, or financial independence number. In the financial industry, the FIN is the accumulation of savings that produce an ongoing income to sustain a retirement lifestyle.

Justin, who considers himself a bit of a math whiz, says, "That's easy. Let me show you"

Annual Income Required	$90,000
Annual Rate of Return	4%
FIN	$2,250,000

"That does look easy," says Jewel, "but why did you pick 4% as the rate of return and $90,000 as our annual income? We make $150,000 and we seem to spend every penny."

"Our banking advisor said that, once our home was paid for and the children were in college, we should only need about 60% of our current income for retirement and that a 4% rate of return was reasonable for retirement savings," says Justin.

Over 2 Million Dollars! That seems like a huge amount, until Justin realizes that this only applies if they never touch the capital. "We would need less if we depleted the money over time," he says. "The bank advisor can help us with that."

"This article says it's more complicated than it looks," points out Jewel, "it says that if we don't consider inflation and, more importantly, taxes, it is very easy to underfund a retirement plan. It also talks about proper diversification of portfolio. Did the banker mention those factors?"

"We didn't go into the details," replies Justin, "but I said we wanted to meet and discuss our mortgage renewal. Why don't we include some retirement planning? Let's make an appointment for next week."

At the meeting, the banker shares the following information:

	Justin	Jewel	Total
After tax income	$76,000	$42,000	$118,000
Current expenses			$116,000
Free cash flow			$2,000
Net monthly income			$9,833
Net monthly expenses			$9,666

As it turns out, Jewel has been stashing away the extra $2,000 in a TFSA at another bank, for a rainy day. She now has just over $10,000 in the account garnering less than 1% interest annually.

Jewel is correct; they are spending almost all of their after tax income. This is not good news. The banker informs them that interest rates have gone up and, although their mortgage has been paid down over the last five years, their previous payment of $2,822 is going to increase to $3,082 to maintain their payout schedule. That will pretty much consume the rainy day fund deposits.

There is some good news. This year, their vehicles will be paid off and that represents almost $1,000 per month. They decide to keep and maintain their current vehicles to free up that cash flow. Also, they are both due for a salary increase, which will net a total of about $5,000 per year.

They decide to commit to a strict budget from now on. Since most of their major expenses are out of the way, there won't be any significant outlays in the near term. With a little belt tightening, they can still manage their annual Hawaii vacation and free up additional income to the tune of $5,000 per year.

All told, they now plan to devote all of their additional income ($22,000) to retirement. It is an aggressive goal but, if all goes well, they should be able to maintain the plan.

Their banker suggests that they each open an RRSP, although Justin should contribute all the funds in the beginning. He has the higher income and a lot of room because they have never contributed. When his limit is reached, the funds will be split and he can then either contribute to a spousal RRSP for Jewel, or, if it makes more sense, she can contribute directly. They will take the tax refund every year and add it to Jewel's Tax-Free Savings Account, or open one in Justin's name and contribute equally to both. The tax refund would amount to approximately $7,050.

The money will be invested in mutual funds inside the RRSP and the TFSA will remain a savings account. The projected rate of return for a balanced mutual fund portfolio is 6% compounded and, for the TFSA, it is 1% over the next twenty years.

To simplify, we will assume one RRSP and one TFSA since it is still legal to income split retirement income from an RRSP.

The Cases' plan to maintain this regimen for twenty years, beginning at age forty and retiring at sixty-five.

Taking into account an extra five years of non-contribution as they wind down their careers, this simplified example yields the following numbers:

RRSP Total Age 65 $1,147,983

TFSA Total Age 65 $177,608

Total After Tax Income: $83,178

Assumption: Both funds are paid out over twenty years to age eighty-five, ending in a zero balance. The tax rate on the RRSP/RIFF money is at 31%. This assumes they split the RRIF income but must still report CPP and OAS income (which we will use to cover inflation).

In this example, the Cases will achieve their original goal: nearly $90,000 of pre-tax income after inflation! This is a perfectly good strategy for retirement. It does depend on the markets being friendly and being able to live with the ups and downs, but a 6% rate of return is very reasonable.

What about estate planning? If their parents do pass at age eighty-five, Crank and Pillow would inherit the family home. Assuming there were no creditors when the will is probated, they could dispose of it tax-free, and split the proceeds - a nice nest egg.

But, what would Crank and Pillow think of a strategy that left them the family home and over *$1 million tax-free*, outside of probate? And, what if that same strategy provided Justin and Jewel with *more* retirement income with no tax burden?

To achieve this result, Justin and Jewel would have to change strategies and consult with advisors outside of the banking industry.

Strategy #1

The (TFSA) is something of a misnomer, tax-free investment account would be more accurate. Whatever its name, the TFSA works best if you can get a solid rate of return, particularly if that return is interest based. Interest income is the highest taxed investment income, but what if we could produce a consistent, above average, interest income in our TFSA? What if, instead of 1%, we obtained a 6% return for the Case family?

Where can we find products that generate that kind of interest income?

In the private equity markets, that's where!

As it turns out, Justin and Jewel just met Maria at a real estate investing course. She is licensed in the exempt market and specializes in private equity investments.

Maria explains that private equity investments are fully regulated and many pay income streams of between 6-12%. They are high-risk investments, however, so most of the Case family savings would have to be in a much safer vehicle such as the one described in Strategy #2.

For now, let's just assume that the Cases invest the annual $7,050 TFSA contribution in private equity and that it returns on average 6%, just like the mutual funds the bank provided. What would be the difference?

Private market investments are not traded on a secondary market so they are less volatile. However, unlike stocks or mutual funds, that can be liquidated virtually the same day, private equity securities require more time to liquidate. Private equity could take weeks, months or even years to redeem so it must be patient money.

If the goal is to compound interest income in a tax-free vehicle until that income is paid out in retirement, some private equity investments, particularly in a TFSA, might be just the ticket. A diversified portfolio using a variety of issuers whose securities are backed by different kinds of assets would help mitigate the risk. A diversified portfolio could include issuers such as:

- ✓ Real Estate
- ✓ Resources
- ✓ Debt Financing
- ✓ Mortgages
- ✓ Other interesting & creative investment strategies, including geographic diversification.

Maria helps the Cases build the portfolio year by year, using the TFSA.

Based on an average 6% rate of return and depleting the funds to zero after 20 years to age eighty-five, this is the result:

TFSA Total $410,795

Total After Tax Income: $33,787

Strategy #2

Maria then suggests a different savings strategy for the remainder of the funds which has the following qualities:

- Guaranteed deposits

- A history of positive returns; over 250 years!

- No market volatility

- Liquidity (guaranteed access to the capital)

- A tax-free income stream at retirement

- A tax-free estate payout to beneficiaries (paid outside of probate)

Although Justin and Jewel are impressed with the private equity plan that Maria has proposed, this new strategy seems too good to be true. Maria convinces them to speak with Randy, an expert on the product.

When they meet, the Cases are surprised to find that Randy is an independent life insurance advisor. How could life insurance possibly be the safe second strategy? Maria assures them that Randy will explain everything.

Randy's explanation goes like this:

There are three types of life insurance available to Canadians.

1. Term Life Insurance

2. Whole Life Insurance

3. Universal Life Insurance

We'll concern ourselves with the first two.

First, let's think about insurance as a protection product. Let's say that insurance is like getting a house to protect our income and assets.

A term insurance contract is like having a rental agreement. The homeowner agrees to allow you to live in the house, if you pay a set amount of rent for a predetermined period. And, when the lease is up, the landlord will renew it, but at a higher cost.

It is the same with term insurance. Typical term policies can run from five to forty years, but most people are acquainted with ten-year or twenty-year term policies. This is because the cost of insurance over time is an exponential curve (see diagram below). That cost curve is set the day an applicant is approved. Of course, like all life insurance, the cost depends on the applicant's age, sex, smoking status, and health. So, although the curve itself is always the same shape, it can travel up and down in terms of cost.

A young, healthy, non-smoking female will be much less expensive to insure than an older, smoking male. Her curve will start lower down the cost coordinate, while his will start much higher. Justin and Jewel are both thirty-nine years old, neither are smokers, and they are both very healthy, but Jewel is still less expensive to insure because she is female. The reason for this is purely statistical – women simply live longer than men, on average.

But, by far, the most interesting fact about the cost of life insurance is the profit calculation.

How much does the insurance company expect to make in profits from the deposits? The answer is: *nothing*! The actuaries who work for the insurance companies try to calculate the exact amount they need to collect in premiums to cover their liability (i.e. the number of claims they will have to pay out). They try to collect only the amount they need to fulfill their policy obligations.

If the insurance company doesn't profit from the deposits, then how do they make money? Well, they collect very large sums that rarely must be paid out all at once and they invest the pool of money. It is their investing prowess that has made life insurance companies among the most respected and profitable financial companies in the world - for over 250 years. They are great at investing.

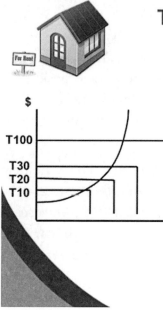

Term Insurance

- Rent Death Benefit (DB):
- Typically No Cash Values
- T10, 20, 30 (Typically Expires Age 85)
- Option - Term to age 100
- DB: Increasing, Decreasing, Level
- Renewable / Convertible to Permanent Insurance
- Typically least expensive <u>immediate</u> premium but can be more expensive to maintain for a lifetime

*m*Powered by NB

Participating Whole Life Policy

Now, let's get back to Strategy #2 and Randy's product, the Participating Whole Life policy. This policy does just what its name implies; it provides insurance coverage for the insured's entire life.

You can think of it like *buying* the house for protection rather than renting. In fact, the insurance company is like the builder of the house. As you make your payments, you build up equity in the house that you can use later.

Like the term policy, the whole life policy must collect enough deposits to cover the statistical liability of future insurance claims, and, since this policy *will* pay out as long as the owner makes the payments, the liability is much greater. Thus, the deposits must be greater as well. The overpayment of premiums accumulates inside the policy and the actuaries know exactly how much this overpayment will be. Therefore, the sums are guaranteed and are written right into the insurance contract. Premiums can also be prepaid, so, in Randy's example to the Cases, the policy will be paid up in twenty years. After that, no more premiums will be required.

The key to this product is the word *participating*. Policy holders get to participate in the profits of the pooled funds invested by the insurance company. Every year, the board of directors uses a proprietary formula to calculate how much of the profit will be shared with policyholders. Over the last twenty-five years, this payout has rivaled the return on the TSX index in Canada, but with one-tenth of the volatility. Policy holders receive an excellent return with no sleepless nights worrying about the markets.

Dividends are paid out in one of four ways:

1) A cash payment (taxable)

2) A reduction in premium deposit for the next year

3) Deposit into the cash value account inside the policy

4) Purchase of more insurance with the balance deposited into the cash value account

These are all good options, but #4 will create the greatest cash value.

Why would you want to buy more insurance every year with the dividend rather than just accumulate it in the cash value account? Because the formula to calculate the annual dividend uses the amount of insurance as one of the factors. The more insurance, the higher the dividend. So, if you increase the amount of insurance every year, your return the next year will be higher. Genius!

But wait! Let's not forget one of the most important features of life insurance. Any money accumulating inside an insurance contract is *tax deferred*. No tax is attributed to the dividend deposits as they accumulate in the cash value account. Wow!

Whole Life Insurance

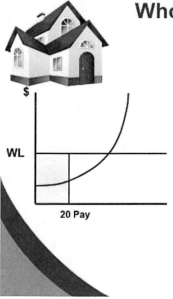

- Buy DB + access to Cash Value during Lifetime (Living Benefits)
- Typically Fixed Deposit Schedule: 20 Pay, or Life Pay
- Option: Participating Policies (Dividends) or Non-Participating
- Investment Component handled by Insurance Company (Bundled)
- Loan Max up to 90% cash value
- GUARANTEES: Level Premium for life, Coverage for Life, Basic Cash Values
- Level guaranteed premiums which can be less expensive overall to maintain for a lifetime

*m*Powered by

So, what do the numbers look like for Justin and Jewel?

Since Randy has replaced their creditor insurance at the bank with personal term life policies for the same price, they are now free to use the Participating Whole Life product as an estate planning tool. This will provide Crank and Pillow Case with that $1 million legacy mentioned earlier.

It will also give Justin and Jewel a safe, tax deferred, savings vehicle for their tax-free retirement income.

Here are the numbers:

Deposit Schedule	$14,950 annually for twenty years (remember, $7,050 goes to TFSA but no tax refund since there is no RRSP contribution).
Initial Insurance Amount	$545,287
Dividend Option	Paid up additional insurance (to get that compounding dividend)
Policy Type	Joint Last to Die (Since this is meant to leave money to kids, no need to pay out until the last parent dies)

At Age 65

Total cash value	$681,752
Total death benefit	$1,222,589
Total fax-Free income	$56,600 (twenty-year payout to age eighty-five)
Estate value at age 85	$1,186,634

"But how is the income tax-free?" asks Jewel. "You said it was only tax deferred as long as it stays inside the cash value account."

"You use the policy as collateral to borrow money from the bank," replies Randy. "Money borrowed from a third party is not taxed."

"Don't we have to pay interest?" says Justin.

"The answer is no," says Randy. "The bank is happy to accumulate the interest payments since it is named as the first beneficiary of the policy. It will collect when the last person passes away, and get paid in thirty days with no estate issues. Banks love this and have been doing it for decades."

"This example," Randy continues, "considers the accumulated interest over the twenty years and the anticipated dividend payouts, along with the accumulated cash value to support the annual loan."

"But, what kind of guarantees do we get with the policy?" says Justin. "The bank tells me that my deposits are 100% guaranteed".

"That's not exactly true," replies Randy. "Bank deposits, such as savings, chequing accounts, or GIC's (five years or less) are insured with the Canada Deposit Insurance Corporation, but only up to a limit of $100,000 per institution. So, if you had $500,000 worth of deposits, you would need accounts at five different banks to be covered. And, bank mutual funds typically have no guarantees at all.

The Participating Whole Life contract, however, has many guarantees:

- ✓ Guaranteed cost of insurance
- ✓ Guaranteed cash value
- ✓ Guaranteed deposit schedule
- ✓ Guaranteed paid up in twenty years
- ✓ Guaranteed policy loan privilege

What is not guaranteed is the annual dividend, but this is not usually an issue. In fact, two top Canadian insurers have carried this product since 1847 and 1920, respectively. Neither has ever missed a dividend. The worst that can happen is that they don't pay the dividend one year. There is no sliding backwards. You cannot lose money, as long as the deposits are paid.

"What happens if the company goes bankrupt?" asks Jewel.

"All Canadian insurance companies belong to a non-profit organization called Assuris. They guarantee the policies and deposits of insurance companies," says Randy. "But, they insure up to 85% of the insurance coverage and deposits of any amount, even if all of your deposits are into one Participating Whole Life policy."

"And if we can't make the payment?" says Justin.

"Then, I would recommend using the TFSA money, but you can also borrow from your own policy to pay the deposit. The contract requires the insurance company to lend you up to 90% of your cash value, no questions asked. In the worst-case scenario, you could collapse the policy and take the cash value. Early on, there would be very little tax to pay, if any, since most of the cash is return of capital."

In the end, Justin and Jewel agree to move forward with an application to see if they qualify.

Conclusion

Based on the numbers below, both retirement strategies contemplated for the Case family would work out very well for them. Their choice would depend largely on their preferences and risk tolerance.

RRSP + TFSA Savings Account Solution

- $83,178 Retirement income
- Estate value – family home

Participating Whole Life + TFSA Private Equity Solution

- $89,787 Retirement income

- Estate value – family home plus $1,186,634 tax-free benefit outside of probate

The real trick for successful retirement planning is to develop a solid financial plan based on time proven strategies and to stick to it. If Canadians start early and make a point of investing for their retirement with regular deposits, then almost any plan will work.

Lessons Learned:

1) Invest sooner. If you can make a habit of investing a minimum of 10% of your income starting as early in adulthood as you can, as long as you don't lose capital, you will accumulate a handsome nest egg, regardless of your rate of return.

2) Negotiate all prices. There is no harm in asking for a reduction, a discount, or a less expensive alternative, no matter what the product or service. See my blog for how to easily create $5,000 of additional income per year just through savvy price negotiation.

3) Ask more questions. The best way to avoid making bad money decisions, or being caught in a financial scam, is to ask more questions. Never, never, and I mean *never* make a spontaneous purchase.

Mindset Tips

1) 90% of success involves just showing up. Try working for one hour a day on your financial well-being. When I was busy with real estate as my side hustle, I would change into work clothes, go to a renovation project every weekday, and promise myself *one hour* of work. One hour only! I could always finish a project using this simple rule.

2) Get independent advice, even if you are an advisor. Most sales programs are designed to shut down our frontal cortex (our ability to reason) as we listen to the offer. This is particularly true when it comes to money. Money is such an emotional subject for most people that they are not equipped to make rational decisions about it. They need a qualified third party to look over the strategy or product for them and provide sound dispassionate advice.

3) Accept your losses with a smile. Sometimes we lose; no investment *always* makes money. That's okay. If we are trying to get better returns for our capital, sometimes we are going to have losses.

Aha Moments and Self Reflections

Note your Thoughts

Blanca Pauliukevicius

Blanca Pauliukevicius, MBA, is a multi-talented entrepreneur, bestselling author, art-tivist, mom, and wife.

She is educated in business and finance and has over twenty years of experience in the private and public sector, where she audited Fortune 500 companies and managed multimillion-dollar budgets and operations.

Blanca is a certified psych-intuitive holistic business coach and Bravery Architect™ for high-achieving, mission-driven entrepreneurs and supports clients in both English and Spanish. She empowers women to heal through mindset shifts in their personal and money stories, align with their soul's purpose and create a brave, joyful and authentic life and profitable business.

Blanca has lived and worked in several continents and is an avid traveler.

Connect with Blanca:

info@blancapauliukevicius.com

Chapter 6

How to Destroy Your Debt, Heal Your Money Story, and Thrive with Health, Wealth and Impact

By Blanca Pauliukevicius

"The rich rule over the poor, and the borrower is servant to the lender."
Proverbs 22:7

Talking about money is taboo for some people—some say it's rude, uncomfortable, or can lead to arguments. Often then, money and debt are the enormous elephant in the room people are happy to pretend isn't there. Everyone is ignoring it, and nobody seems to want to talk about it. However, money problems are a leading factor destroying marriages, dreams and even taking lives. If we don't start talking about it, confronting it honestly and managing it, debt can be devastating. Confronting money issues can also be incredibly healing and empowering when we take back control instead of letting it control us.

Yet, I get it. I understand why talking about money is so taboo. It makes you confront the person in the mirror: you, your habits, maybe even some of your mistakes. Sometimes you might even completely avoid talking or thinking about, or even acting on debt and other financial issues.

Precisely because money is such a large issue in our lives, it is vital that we get honest and talk about it. Being open about money issues will strip it of its power over us, and put us back in the driver's seat.

One of the biggest issues many of us face with money has to do with debt. From credit cards and student loans to medical bills and other expenses, debt seems to be looming over far too many people, leading to extreme stress and limiting our lives. This behavior, called *indebtedness*, comes from childhood and self-limiting beliefs, from our core needs and values. We need to understand it in order for us to get control of it and channel it to healthy levels.

To do this, I want to share my perspective on this issue of debt and money management. I will share how to shift your mindset so you can get rid of your debt and start saving for your future, and I want to share with you the tactics that worked for me to get out of over $180,000 in debt.

The American Dream

Let's begin by examining the core of the money mindset of so many Americans. We are brainwashed everyday with billions of dollars spent on advertising, attempting to convince us that debt is glamorous, and that you can get your version of the "American Dream" on credit. A flashy lifestyle is presented as possible in a matter of a few payments; a dream lifestyle that most people cannot afford to pay in cash.

We are trying to 'keep up with the Joneses'', the neighbors up the hill with the big house, new cars, designer clothes... and very likely a whole lot of debt. But we don't think about that part, we are encouraged to buy everything on credit—the car, the furniture, the new gadgets, the toys, and once we get out of control we start buying our basic needs on credit, too. Talk about rapidly depreciating stuff. Worse yet, most times we don't pay these credit cards off at the end of the month, so we end up carrying over the balance, month after month, in the name of cash flow.

I am not saying that getting all of these nice things is bad, in fact it can be great. It feels so right when you can afford to pay for life and occasional luxuries in cash, and when you are not getting into debt and paying high interest in the process. That is just not wise financially, and that's when debt starts piling up and can start causing major problems in your life.

"When you are content to be simply yourself and don't compare or compete, everyone will respect you."
- Tao Te Ching: *A New English Version by Stephen Mitchell*

The Culture of Debt

The culture of debt is a powerful and popular culture. I am not here shaming anyone or myself for succumbing to this culture or these habits. It is important to understand how we are led here and how our behaviors play into the problem so that we can address this madness and stop it.

I understand that not everyone joins in the culture of debt, but a vast number of us do. I know I did, and it got ugly.

A big part of the culture leads us to overworking in an effort to keep up with all our debt, or to fulfill a desire to acquire more. We work longer hours or extra jobs or pick up a side hustle, but not to save or to get ahead. We work these long hours to try to keep from sinking.

In a study compiled by the economic thinktank Washington Center for Equitable Growth, they looked at why we're putting in such long hours, along with the economic and health effects of overwork. They concluded that rising economic inequality lead to the culture of overwork.

It's a vicious circle of consumerism, overworking, and getting in debt. In America this is one of the easiest things to do because our financial system and economy encourages it. It's also toxic for your financial future and your health. It is so engrained in our culture that once you enter the debt system you must keep going to survive. Or so we think.

"Possessions, outward success, publicity, luxury— to me these have always been contemptible. I believe that a simple and unassuming manner of life is best for everyone, best for both the body and the mind."
- Albert Einstein

The Debt and Wealth Relationship

Debt is thought by many to be seen as a "tool" to create wealth. Early on, when I first arrived in the U.S., I got my real estate license. I was taught that using other people's money was good, in the form of debt in relation to investments. However, there's more to that story few will tell you, and that has to do with the risks involved in getting into debt without the ability to fully repay that debt and respond to fluctuations in the economy or even your own personal financial circumstances.

When the economy takes a downturn or you lose your job, or your investment is upside down or the worst-case-scenario—all of these things happen at the same time, and you can't give the property away fast enough, and you don't have the emergency savings to keep paying while in transition, you lose everything. Your finances tank. Your credit tanks. Your sense of security and even self-worth tanks. Your stress levels rise, and often your health and mental health are at risk. Now, you are left in crisis with a terrible financial, emotional and health crash that can take years, even decades to sort out, heal from and get stable again.

There is a healthy relationship between debt and wealth, but it requires savings and cash flow to balance out the risk of the debt. Too often, that last part is left out of the equation, and countless people are left vulnerable.

Getting Out of the Pit of Debt

In 2008, the worst-case-scenario is exactly what happened to me and millions of people who bought into real estate just before the market crashed. I managed to get myself into my version of the "American Dream" with over $330,000 in debt. $240,000 of that was personal investment in real estate, and some other expenditures. In my attempt to recover from a divorce, *stabilize* myself in this country, and get my own home, I fell into the trap that the majority of Americans fall into. I spent way more than I could afford and was living way beyond my income.

As life would have it, I got laid off and the economy crashed. I got into way too much risky debt, but not enough funds saved as a backup. I found myself in over $180,000 of debt after clearing the mortgage debt with the Debt Forgiveness Act. Most of that debt was charged off, so it was also considered taxable revenue, which left me in a pickle with the IRS too.

I eventually landed a great job, and at that point I had been working my way out of debt. I had saved enough to cover my liabilities and settle my debts without filing for bankruptcy. This took extreme focus and discipline and some savings, and it certainly *dinged* my credit. I had worked very hard to have good credit, so this was devastating. It also happened to be the best thing for me, because it made me realize how I was relating to money; how I was not tracking it or respecting it.

All of this lead me to becoming very in-touch with my finances, and I worked my way out of debt. I soon learned that debt is not, in fact, a good tool to create wealth. Many wealthy people have built their wealth using their income, cash instead of credit.

I began to understand that the greatest source of wealth is the income I make. I know now how to use it to make it grow for me via compounded interest and other forms of investment. But, if I just use my money to spend it, I will not accumulate wealth, I will accumulate *stuff* and debt.

> *"My wealth has come from a combination of living in America, some lucky genes, and compound interest."*
> - Warren Buffett

> *"The most important financial decision of your life needs to be made right now! It's time for you to decide to become an investor, not just a consumer."*
> - Tony Robbins, MONEY, Master the Game: 7 Simple Steps to Financial Freedom

How Debt Works

In order to manage debt, you really need to understand it—how the financial industry works, and why it depends on you being in debt for it to make money off of you.

Money was originally created as a tool to facilitate trade. Today, we have assigned such an immense power to money that it can rule our lives. The power and meaning we give to money very much determines how we live. Some people have even done horrifying things for money: suicide, kidnapping, terrorism, and murder. More commonly, it has torn apart families and businesses, has kept people sick, and lead to feelings of worthlessness.

In the best scenarios, we learn that what matters most has nothing to do with money: our health, the people in our lives, etc. When we fully acknowledge this, having a balanced relationship with money is far easier to attain. Our capacity to adapt our emotional needs with our material possessions reflects how our values and desires are prioritized in our world.

Meanwhile, the messages we receive from American culture opposes this balance. Debt is a product, and the credit card industry spends billions of dollars annually in marketing and reward offers convincing us to get more credit cards. Americans were projected to surpass $4,000 trillion in consumer debt in December 2018, according to the Consumer Credit Release from Federal Reserve.

Consumer Debt Statistics (from creditdonkey.com)

- About 77% of American households have debt of some kind

- The average credit card debt is $5,331

- 83% of adults have at least one credit card

- 55% of credit card users don't always pay their balance in full

- The average credit cards per person is 3.1

- The current outstanding revolving debt in the U.S. is $1.04 trillion

- The average APR on credit card accounts assessed interest is %16.46

- Baby Boomers and Generation X have the most debt

So, evidently, we are not winning at this game of indebtedness. Far too many of us are living way beyond our income thanks to the big industry of debt.

> *"We buy things we don't need with money we don't have to impress people we don't like."*
> - Dave Ramsey, *The Total Money Makeover: A Proven Plan for Financial Fitness*

Debt-Healthy Mindset

An important part of a debt-healthy mindset begins with understanding that when we heal our past and our self-worth, our relationship with ourselves, our money, and the people in our lives changes. Psychological studies show that spending is emotional, and when we start noticing our behavior, we can start to make changes. Let's start with stopping before we buy, noticing how we feel and asking questions:

1) What is it that I really need right now?

2) Why am I feeling this way?

3) Then ask why again…and again until you get to them bottom of the reason for the impulse.

4) Make sure to journal about this. There is something about releasing that energy on paper that is so cathartic.

5) Then find a way to satisfy the deepest need behind the impulse. Usually the solution is emotional, something unrelated to spending money. E.g. taking a walk or meeting a friend to talk and just connect.

Note: *How we think and feel about money or our old stories sometimes sabotage our attempts to make good decisions about our money.* Yet, even when we make mistakes, we get to go back and choose to make better decisions and continuously improve our financial design.

To curb impulse spending ask yourself these questions:

- Do I really *need* this or do I just want it?

- Do I already own one?

- If I say yes to this, what am I saying no to? (be mindful of your budget)

- Can I make do with something else or is this *absolutely* essential that I buy it?

- Is it the right time, or what would be the worst that can happen if I don't buy this right now?

Before you make a purchase outside of basic necessities, from now on, run through this spending checklist, and you will see how you curb your spending.

"Personal Finance is 80% behavior and 20% head knowledge."
- Dave Ramsey

Next, think deeper about mindset, and how you define success. Is it money or something bigger? What does success mean to you?

My definition of success is to be able to reach my goals and passion projects. Where I can have a positive impact in the life of other people and those around me, and where my daily activities bring me joy, freedom, adventure, and I can be self-reliant and have financial stability.

Ask yourself these other questions to help further explore what success means to you and to better shape your mindset:

1) What do you value?

2) Think of times you were happiest?

3) Remember times you were the proudest? What made you proud?

4) What made you feel fulfilled and satisfied? What was so memorable?

Money and Our Emotions

Our spending behaviors are a great window into our relationship with money.

Most people were taught how to relate to money early in life. We saw what was modeled to us by our parents, by the way they handled their money or lack thereof and this informed our money story. Our behavior, compulsive or not, comes from a deep-seated issue about our money story from childhood, a scarcity mindset, guilt for having too much, or our innate tendency to seek instant gratification.

Ask Yourself:

- What did you learn about your money story from your parents?

- How did these stories impact your beliefs about money?

- Do your current beliefs support your values?

- What do you think about spending money, about tracking and investing money?

- What do you believe about rich people, and poor people?

- What would support you in building a new money story for you and your family?

We must go back to our childhood years to find out how our parent's beliefs about money affected us, how their behaviors influenced our abilities, perceptions and expectations. Then we must own our part in all of this.

As adults, we also have to take responsibility for our own choices. So, a good exercise in self-awareness is asking yourself, for every statement you think or say that your money problems were someone else's fault, what really was your part in that?

1) Does thinking of having plenty of money or not having enough money bring up feelings of sadness, anger, worry, anxiety, power, love or joy?

2) Did your parents fight about money? Did they use it as a form of control? Conversely, was it used as a way to show love?

3) Did you grow up humbly, in a household were money was scarce? Or were your parents wealthy or financially secure? What were the money beliefs your parents or authority figures in your lives modeled to you?

Journal:

Think about all these memories and start journaling how you felt, and see if there are similar feelings when you make a purchase or avoid investing or avoid learning more to improve your finances. See where the resistance comes from.

It takes tremendous focus to end the cycle of being in debt, strong emotions, *Motivation And Discipline (MAD)*. To get out of debt you have to get *MAD*. Dave Ramsey states in his book *Financial Peace University*, "Get mad!!! There is no energy in logic, only emotion. When you get ticked off you can get out. Years of counseling have revealed that this plan works. You can't scheme, scam, or borrow your way out of debt. You just have to get mad."

You are tracing new neural pathways in your brain when you engage in new focused behaviors. At first, it will be hard. Ensure you make it rewarding for yourself when you take little positive steps, such as only paying by card if it is your debit card. Just make sure the reward doesn't involve spending money. You can maybe take yourself on a beautiful stroll somewhere you love, or spend an afternoon reading, find something you love that brings you joy. The best first step, I would say, is to just use cash and track it on your budget sheet.

You should also note or journal how you are feeling when you track your money, if you find resistance or neglect to track it and when you are spending money. These emotions will reflect to you if you have a dysfunctional relationship with money. For the most part, if we don't manage it, track it or respect it, we don't master it, we don't feel safe nor powerful in our financial lives. Our relationship with money is like any other relationship that needs healthy boundaries, honesty and ongoing positive actions towards a goal. So, you must dig down to the root of the problem in order to make consistent positive changes, acknowledge our mistakes and repair the relationship by giving it the care and attention we give to any of our important relationships in life.

Benefits of Living Debt Free

Something I know for certain, when you are debt free, can pay off your credit card spending every month, and have savings to weather any worst-case-scenario financial struggle, you are sure to be:

1) Healthier—reduced stress, better sleep, etc., plus you can afford better health care.

2) Eating better food— you can afford healthier food choices vs. processed and fast foods that are poisoning us.

3) Having better relationships—increased openness, support, reduced financial tension, and relaxation in business and life.

4) Self-sufficient—no need to stay in a bad relationship for financial reasons.

5) Working reasonable hours—no need to work extra hours to keep up with debt, which could lead to more quality time with family and friends.

6) Able to provide more security for your family—afford better neighborhoods where your children can live safer lives; support your family and loved ones in their dreams and needs without stress.

7) Able to impact the world positively by showing up as powerful, confident and in control. You are in a position to help others who are in need of support to rise up, and may even see you as an inspiring role model.

Having no debt is a very counter-culture idea. A significant number of Americans who have credit cards don't think they will ever be completely be free of credit card debt. Yet, with strategy, commitment and work it is a totally achievable goal. There *is no* better feeling than being debt free!

Steps to Becoming Debt Free

These are some of the steps I took to get rid of debt without filing for bankruptcy. Always consult with a lawyer about your particular situation; this is not intended to be used directly as financial or legal advice. I used the debt snowball plan from Dave Ramsey's *Financial Peace University* to get out of debt, and I am following the baby steps to financial freedom. I highly recommend his plan and books for further details.

Dave Ramsey's 7 Baby Steps to Financial Freedom:

1) Save a $1000 emergency fund

2) Pay off debt by using the snowball method

3) Build a three-sixth month fund

4) Invest 15% of your gross household income in retirement plans (401K, 403b's with match then Roth IRAs, make sure you have adequate insurance and a $500-$1000 deductible

since you now have the savings to drastically lower your premiums)

5) Start a college savings fund

6) Pay off your mortgage

7) Give, make donations

"Beware of little expenses, a small leak will sink a great ship."
- Benjamin Franklin

Some Ways to End Debt That Worked for Me:

- Draft a lean budget and stick with it. There are many useful budgeting systems, just make sure you account for every dollar that goes out.

- If possible, find an accountability partner to help you stay on track.

- Review your budget weekly and identify areas to cut back. E.g. excess, subscriptions, cable (I don't watch TV), eating out, entertainment and experiences switched to free options.

- Consider a spending freeze on clothing and travel.

- Cut up credit cards.

- Start saving like your life depends on it, because it does!

- Write to the credit bureau and request discrepancies to be erased within 30 days. By law if they cannot send you proof of the debt, they must take it off. Make sure you follow up in 30 days of your receipt confirmation. You can google sample letters for credit bureau.

- Save some money that cannot be easily spent, and don't touch it at all except for emergencies.

- Consider using prepaid legal service and hire lawyers to help negotiate with banks or provide direction on any lawsuits brought up due to bad debts, as in most cases you are personally responsible for the debts.

- Sell stuff around your house that you don't need and apply it to your debt.

- Use any cash savings (except for your emergency savings) to negotiate your debts, and save some money to pay for the taxes on the charged off debt.

- Whenever possible, use 0% credit cards to transfer balances with zero transfer fees and tackle them to pay them off as soon as possible.

- (Note: The banks/credit card companies never lose; they charge the debt off on your credit, but they still claim the loss with the IRS, and you will get taxed on that portion of unpaid debt as income to you.)

Tip: Money management isn't all about savings and reduced spending—the other half is about increasing your income to afford the lifestyle you want along with what you need.

Some Creative Ways to Earn Extra Income:

- Google creative ways to raise or earn money. You will find a myriad of ways to make extra cash, it will blow your mind. This resource was not there when I was trying to get out of debt.

- Find ways to make extra cash online, make a course that you can sell online, get a side gig, do some freelancing (check out the platform Upwork.com), tutoring, translation, or doing anything that you are good at, that people can pay you money for, then apply all that income directly to debt-reduction.

- Right now, you can sign up with UBER, turn on the app on your way home or any long distance and drive people or deliver food while you commute home. You can make a few hundred dollars a month that way.

Living Debt Free Resources

After four tight years, I was *debt free*. It was very hard, very stressful to go through this debt crisis, but I got through it and I learned the lesson, and about myself in the process. It was the most freeing thing I have ever done for myself. There is nothing that brings more calm, ease and level-headiness than making decisions from a place of unencumbered freedom. If you want more resources you can download my *Get Rid of Debt Checklist* for Free here: www.braveryarchitect.com/freebies

I am not financial advisor, and I only talk from my experience, from what I learned and what I value. Although, after what I have been through and what I have been learning, I might just become a professional financial advisor in the future. But in the meantime, you can find a financial advisor here: http://findanadvisor.napfa.org/

We are *all* on this journey, perhaps at different stages, but we are all healing from limiting beliefs and behaviors that aren't serving us. So, in sharing some of my discoveries here with you I hope that it inspires you to change and take control, to show up confident, positive and powerful about your future.

> *"Wealth consist not in having great possessions,*
> *but in having few wants."*
> - Epictetus

Lessons Learned:

1) Question your money mindset, your values and why owning something is important to you.

2) Track your spending plan/budget weekly at the very least. Make it a habit, get *MAD* to get out of debt.

3) Follow a financial freedom plan, so you know in advance where your money is going to go, you will be more likely to follow through.

Mindset Tips:

1) Believe in yourself. With a clear plan, consistency and creativity, you *will* be debt free. Shift your money stories by digging into your past to understand why you relate to money the way you do, and repair the relationship with money to one of respect and care.

2) Don't dwell on shame or mistakes. Learn from your errors, forgive yourself and keep going with your freedom from debt plan.

3) Build a new money story by journaling and sharing throughout your debt free efforts. A strong new story will outshine the old story that wasn't serving you.

Aha Moments and Self Reflections

Note your Thoughts

Todd D. Schmekel

Todd has an M.Ed. in Leadership and Teaching from the University of Calgary and has completed the Canadian Securities Course as well as numerous other courses in investment and finance. At fourteen, Todd first became interested in investing when he entered a national newspaper's Stock Market Challenge. From that day on, he was hooked and for a time, he made his living as a day-trader.

In 2014, Todd went through a major life change, leaving a career of over twenty years in education and getting divorced. He knows that when investors experience life-changing events or simply lack time, their financial lives can often unravel. They may rely on hope to solve their financial issues rather than implementing a solid plan.

Todd currently lives with his wife and two daughters and operates a successful financial advisory practice in Calgary. Investments have always been an important part of Todd's life, but his passion is helping people overcome their obstacles on the path to financial freedom.

Connect with Todd:

todd.schmekel@edwardjones.com

Chapter 7

When All Your Eggs Fall Out of the Basket

By Todd D. Schmekel

"Your beliefs become your thoughts, your thoughts become your words, your words become your actions, your actions become your habits, your habits become your values, your values become your destiny."
-Mahatma Gandhi

In 2013 I was smart. Really smart. And I had plenty of evidence to prove that fact. At work, I was at the top of my game. I'd been in education for more than twenty years. Like most, I'd started as a teacher, but I didn't stay in the profession for long. I'd been ambitious and quickly moved through the ranks landing in the principalship of the largest schools. They became successful educationally, culturally, and financially. Soon I was moving from one school jurisdiction to the next. Always assigned to a school in crisis, a school that was failing. My role was transformation, and I excelled in my position. I left each school with a solid educational plan in place, happy students, productive staff and a vision for the future.

My home life wasn't much different. I'd been married for nearly twenty-five years. We'd always been busy, both as educators, and I was also an entrepreneur. I started a technology company because I wanted a challenge, and in the early 1990s technology seemed to be cropping up everywhere. Cell phones were becoming common place, computers were making their way into classrooms, and small business and I didn't want to be left behind. I wanted to be a leader.

Everything fell into place, and life was easy. We got regular raises at work, I got promotions and pay increases, and although we didn't need the extra money that I earned in technology, it did allow us a lifestyle that a few short years before had seemed impossible. We took trips. We bought. We became debt free. We saved. We dreamed.

Our future looked bright, so we took the plunge and started a family. First one beautiful daughter and then another. They were—and are—perfect.

Suddenly, we were a typical family. We did what good parents do. We gave our kids opportunities: dance, sports, music, language education, and family trips. We also made sure that we wouldn't become 'those' parents. You know, the ones that save nothing for their retirement. There was no way we were going to become those parents whose retirement is spent crowded into their children's spare bedroom under the pretense that they'd rather be helping raise their grandchildren than live out their golden years in style. We wanted to be parents that helped with mortgages, took our extended family on paid vacations, and lent money to our kids to avert crisis. So, we saved. We maximized our Registered Retirement Plans (RRSP) and our Tax-Free Savings Accounts (TFSA); we paid off our mortgage and reveled in the fact that we were public servants with Defined Benefit Pension Plans. We did one more thing. We invested. Our financial future looked bright.

Education had gotten us to where we were, and we knew it. In those days, I had dreams of becoming a father to a doctor, a lawyer or a veterinarian. My wife didn't care. A hairstylist or barista was fine as long as the girls chose a career that made them happy. That was never ambitious enough for me, never secure enough for me. We agreed on what was most important; that our girls would have a future of opportunity. We would not allow student debt to define their lives as it had ours in the early years of our careers and marriage. We started a Registered Education Savings Plan (RESP); we maximized our contributions. Again, we invested.

Are you beginning to see how smart I was? Others also noticed. I got an executive promotion at work, a raise, a secondary pension plan, and finally the opportunity to do things my way. A chance to shape teaching, student learning, and school leadership. It was what I'd been waiting for; I was a superintendent. Things were naturally falling into place. My wife found a teaching position around the corner from our home and in the same school that our youngest daughter attended. If there was anything amiss at that time, it was that my wife didn't enjoy her job. Yet she seemed to accept that what we were building required her to work. To be honest, we didn't spend much time together, and I didn't take her complaints very seriously. We were going to have to work hard for the good life we wanted.

Our relationship wound up falling on life support. We'd married young and had developed separate interests, career aspirations, and friends. Most of our time together was chasing after kids and going to family events. This struck me as pretty normal.

Then in December 2014, I screwed everything up. I wasn't so smart after all. What I was, was profoundly unhappy.

Sure, I had some help. But sometimes you have to just man up and accept your mistakes and the consequences that go with them. What happened, you're wondering? Why was I unhappy? Where should I start?

At work, I'd gotten a new CEO. From the outset, there was conflict between us. He was about buses, budgets, and buildings whereas I was about programs for kids, quality of teaching and improving leadership. We were different. Not better. Just different, but it was obvious we couldn't work together.

By December of that year, I knew I had to leave. He wanted me gone, and if the truth be known, I needed to go. Although I'd worked nearly my entire professional life to get to where I was, I accepted an offer to buy-out the remainder of my contract. Looking back, I don't really know how I felt. Scared? A bit. Sad? Somewhat. Excited? Not at all. Mostly, I was in shock. The situation at work was bad, and my home life was no better. By the end of the year, I found myself unemployed living alone in a small condo and needing a family lawyer.

I was angry that all I'd done for the last school division had been ignored and forgotten. I was bitter that people I'd thought of as colleagues and friends stopped calling and ignored my invitations. But what really made me seethe was the realization that any job in education would mean leaving my kids behind. I'd have to move to a different city. I knew the drill. I'm a child of divorce, and I was well aware of the impact separation has on the father-child relationship. I took a stand and decided I wasn't leaving my kids. It was the first time in my life I'd put my career second. Was I learning? Was I finally getting my priorities straight?

I was luckier than most who find their lives turned upside down. I had some time, not a lot, but some. My contract buy-out gave me an opportunity. First, it gave me enough money to live on for a while and second, it gave me a number of hours of counseling. I can only assume that the counseling hours are included in severance packages to help with potential depression and to assuage any feelings of guilt on the part of the past employer should ex-employees do something rash. I chose a different path. I invested the counseling hours with a psychologist who focused on career counseling. Megan was fabulous (not her real name, of course).

Her first order of business was to uncover why I wanted a career change. Then, she held me accountable for my mistakes and refused to allow me to blame others or rationalize away poor judgment. We talked, she listened, but most of all we investigated what I might do to get back on my feet.

"What are you good at?" she asked.

"At this point, I'm not really sure," I responded.

"Then, what are you passionate about?"

"No idea," I said with a hint of sarcasm, thinking Dr. Phil may have taken over my session. I wasn't interested in what I was passionate about. I needed a job.

"You need to find the answers to these questions."

"Why? How do I do that? And don't tell me it's yoga or I that need to align my chakras or I'm out of here." I'm a bit of a skeptic and even more sarcastic. Megan had uncovered my superpower.

"How about we start with a personality inventory?" It was less a question, and more of a 'this is how we do things' statement, so I went along.

The results were unsurprising. I enjoyed helping others. True. I had some leadership skills. Okay, that was likely an off-shoot from my career. I had a knack for making the complex simple. I guess so. I could be skeptical and sarcastic. We'd already discovered that fact. I like being alone, and I have a decent sense of humor. Don't we all? As far as I was concerned, I was getting no closer to the job I desperately needed.

"So, what kind of career do you think these traits best suit you for?" Megan asked.

"Sounds like teaching to me."

"Do you want to be a teacher? Go back to a career in education?"

"Nope, but I have no idea what else I can do with my experience, my qualifications, and my aptitude. It's all I've ever done." Unknown to Megan, I'd become a junkie of the employment website Indeed.com. I'd applied for numerous jobs that I thought my experience and credentials were a good match for, all outside of education, all without a single call or interview. Turns out our education credentials and a Masters Degree in Education aren't much valued in the employment market.

"How about we do another test? The kind that matches personality traits and interests to career opportunities? There are over 40,000 occupations in the world. Let's see what we uncover."

The results of this test were surprising. Sure, education was on the list of the top ten careers I might enjoy, but it was number eight. What really caught my eye was that finance was number one. What did that mean? I'd grown up with a banker for a mother, and I didn't see running a bank, being a bank teller or a loan's officer as my cup of tea.

"What stands out for you in the results?" Megan asked.

"First, that education is so far down the list. And second, that finance is number one. I enjoy trading stocks in my discount brokerage account, but I certainly don't want to be a banker or an accountant. Being trapped in a room with a spreadsheet is not my idea of a good time."

"What did you just say you enjoyed?" asked Megan

"Ah…trading stocks and investing, I guess. I like doing research on companies. Finding out what's a good buy and what's not so good. I think I've worked hard in life and I like my money to do some of the heavy lifting. When I was married, I had a pretty good plan for retirement, for holidaying and we were completely out of debt. That's not the case now. Investing is really just a hobby."

"You sound pretty excited about *just* a hobby."

"I guess. To be honest, since I left education, I've been actively following markets, reading the about the greats of the investment world, like Warren Buffett, and using what I've learned where I think it makes sense. Problem is my divorce didn't leave me with a lot."

"Okay, that's it for our session for today, your homework for our next session is to find out a little more about the top three of the occupation categories we've uncovered and the qualifications you might need to enter these fields. Okay?" said Megan.

I didn't do it. I tried. I went back to Indeed.com. I searched jobs in finance and I got stuck there. As I looked up the financial advisor category, financial planner, retirement specialist, and other similar positions kept catching my eye. They sounded interesting. I read the qualifications. I had none. *How could I get them*, I wondered? I became a spy.

When Monday morning came around, I called and clandestinely visited a number of the companies on the list, posing as a potential client. Knowing what I know now, I should have become a client; it would have saved me a lot of money in the short-term. I set about to interview the people I met. What products did they offer? What could they guarantee me? What experience did they have? How did they decide to take a job in finance? Where did they get their qualifications? I thanked each of them for their help and said I'd call back. I didn't. Spies don't call back.

Instead, I enrolled in the Canadian Securities Course. I figured that even if I didn't pursue a career in finance, what I learned would make me a better investor. I figured if I'd earned a Masters in Leadership, then some facts and figures about investing shouldn't be too difficult. But I was always conscious of the time—I needed a job. I completed the first course in a few months. I took another and then another and soon I was, on paper at least, qualified to become a financial advisor. I learned a lot and then I had learned some more. And all the while I was learning, I was getting that icky feeling. The more I learned, the more my case of the 'ickies' grew. My investments were a mess! They'd been a mess forever and I was only now just beginning to understand how much trouble I was in.

My now ex-wife and I had been investors, and we had an advisor that we met with once a year. He suggested mutual funds, segregated funds, and a new type of insurance product that I now recognize as Universal Life. He recommended, we agreed, and we bought. We figured that that's how the process worked. He lived in the same small town we did, and though we didn't know him, others seemed to trust him, so we did as well. What we were buying and how his recommendations were determined was never really clear, but we like the names of the products. Growth, balanced, and dividend were all terms that sounded sophisticated, and others like load and deferred sales charge just sounded like nonsense. It really didn't matter that we didn't understand them; *he* understood. We never once asked how much it cost for him to take care of us, we assumed it was fair and he had our best interests at heart. It all made sense; we were in the big leagues now, we were investors. We had an advisor.

We had also started a small discount brokerage account, so we could try our hand at stocks. I managed our investments and I bought some penny stock. Mostly in companies I'd heard about from friends, neighbors and the guys on my hockey team. My accountant told me about a micro-mining company in British Columbia that was going to "hit it big." I was considering buying some shares in TD Bank. Instead, I bought the micro-miner. Only a fool wouldn't want to "hit it big." Everyone knew about the banks, but only a select few of us got the tip about the micro-miner. When I could, I started watching a weekly TV program where experts gave away their best advice on stocks for free. I bought some of those as well. Investing really boiled down to being first. Getting the tip first, getting an expert opinion first and buying before others did and then selling when they bought.

Unfortunately, most of those companies went out of business. And in that ten-year period when I passed up TD for that now defunct micro-miner, TD grew nearly 100%. We lost money, but it didn't affect our day-to-day lives, and it gave us something to boast about with friends and family. Everyone talks up their winners and forgets their losers. We never considered how it might affect our future. But after becoming a financial advisor, I know that it did and more than I'd like to admit.

I went through my divorce settlement, and this was when I began to wonder what I'd done to my financial future. In our divorce settlement, I came away with our discount brokerage, part of a TFSA, an RRSP, half of my children's RESP and a portion of my teacher's pension. I'd made a lot more money than my ex-wife and in order to balance our assets she got the house and a significant part of my pension. This was when I first began to wonder what I'd done to my financial future, but emotions were high, and the lawyers were at war with one another.

I'd always been a meticulous record keeper. I started to apply what I was learning to my old investment statements. I was less shocked by what I found. In ten years, I'd made virtually nothing. Why had I been put in these investments? Of course, hindsight is twenty-twenty, and this is particularly true when reviewing investment returns. It's always much easier to pick the winners when you know them in advance. I decided to set performance aside. Instead, I focused on whether or not the investments were fit for me. I reviewed what I'd learned, started the process, and then it happened. I got a job.

It happened just in time. Sure, I needed the money, but what it really did was take my understanding of investing to the next level. The in-house training was fantastic. The tools, superb. The access to investment research unheard of. I'd learned about risk tolerance, portfolio construction, volatility, tax efficiency, time horizon, asset allocation, the importance of a plan, and many other fundamental tools of the investment world. I learned how they worked together and how to apply them to each person's unique situation. It was work, but it was work with purpose.

In the evening, when I wasn't in training, I stayed late. I applied what we'd done that day and the information from my studies to my portfolio. The icky feeling came back. In ten years of a very good market, I'd done poorly. I did a risk questionnaire and discovered that knowing an investor's risk tolerance is as important as knowing one's shoe size. We all need and want investments that fit who we are. Investments that help us reach our goals, but still let us sleep at night. I'd never done a risk tolerance with my advisor, and that probably explained why my investments were in conservative mutual funds when I was willing to accept a more growth-focused approach. In part, it explained why I'd been invested in a portfolio more suited for a retiree than a professional in the prime of their earning years.

Later that week, I entered the numbers and investments from my post-divorce statements into the firm's planning software. The icky feeling loomed again, this time it became suffocating. Based on the assets I had and the investments I was using I could retire at sixty-five with the same monthly income of the guy who delivered my Friday night pepperoni pizza (If you're a pizza delivery guy and make a lot of money you should invest and don't be offended by that last statement. Instead get my pizza guy a job at your place. He's a good guy, but he's broke.) No way. That was not going to work. I didn't spend twenty-five years as a professional to retire in poverty. I needed a plan.

I redid my risk tolerance. It came out the same. I considered my time horizon. It was fifteen years, maybe twenty. I reviewed my investments, my income, and my ability to save on a monthly basis. I asked the tough questions. Was I willing to work longer than sixty-five? Could I do a better job of budgeting and then start saving again? Was I spending money irresponsibly? When should I take my Canada Pension (CPP) and how much might it be? Would I qualify for Old Age Security (OAS)? How much would my teacher's pension pay in retirement and what could I reasonably expect my investments to provide. Good financial data is the foundation of every financial plan.

Based on my risk tolerance, time horizon, and my life stage, my asset allocation changed. I chose investments that not only fit who I was as an investor, but those that also had been reviewed and recommended by the firm's research team. I'd never heard of many of them and based on my experience I was skeptical of investment recommendations. I reviewed the recommendations that had been made ten years ago. How had they done? Much better than I had. History may not be able to predict the future, but at least I knew the recommendation process had some merit. I learned about costs and how to balance them against value. My mantra became, "Cost isn't everything, but it's not nothing either."

I grimaced at the deferred sales charges that had eaten up so much of my capital when we were forced to sell mutual funds to complete the financial settlement of my divorce. These costs came without value in my opinion. However, it all slowly came together and voila: I had a plan. It was flexible, but it was clear and concise. The plan was based on who I was and who I wanted to become, and I knew if I followed it, I had an excellent chance of reaching my financial goals, including retirement.

It is often said that bad things come in threes. I can solidly identify my job loss and divorce at the same time as two of those things. The third is a bit more elusive. I'm not sure if was finding out that people who were my friends at work turned out not to be friends at all when I needed them most, or the realization that employers didn't see my experience as particularly valuable. I think it's also true that when you are at your lowest, you are also in the best position to sit back and think about what got you to that position. Like most of us, I had plenty of blame to go around. When the blaming is done, and the crying is over you really only have one choice: to pick yourself up, get going, and make a new life in any way you can. No one else is going to do it for you, and that's probably good. It's your job. It's your life.

One evening, I went on a date. She seemed to know what she wanted out of her life. She must have thought I'd given birth to a baby and named him Financial Plan based on my rambling on about investments. We talked:

"So, your plan is finally done? You've certainly put a lot of work into it?" she asked.

"Yeah, I have, but it was a good learning experience. If I'm going to help people reach their financial goals, I better have some skin in the game and be willing to practice what I preach," I said as I poured us another glass of wine.

"So, you're going to be rich soon?"

"Ha, not likely. What I'm going to be is okay, if I can just work out one more kink."

"Oh? What's the kink?" she questioned.

"Saving. I just can't stick to a budget. I don't have the will power. At the end of the month, I've got nothing left and haven't saved a dime. Planning doesn't mean saving," I moaned.

"I don't think saving means planning either," she said.

"Huh?"

"It seems to me that you might be looking at this the wrong way."

"Oh?"

"What if you saved first and spend second? Could that work?" she asked.

"You mean pay yourself first, like Dave Chilton says in the Wealthy Barber?"

"I don't know who David Chilton is, and I certainly don't know any rich hair stylists, but you've got the idea."

"That could work. That's perfect. Each month I'll pay myself exactly what I need to save to reach my goals and then I'll spend the rest. When I run out, I won't be stressed about not having saved, and my plan will work."

The final piece was in place. I didn't know it at the time, but working on my plan, understanding my risk tolerance, and learning about investments allowed me to stop feeling sorry for myself. It freed me. I was no longer paralyzed by the changes in my life and the mindset that I had no future because of what I'd lost. My belief that I was a financial and personal ruin was a lie. Is that what you believe? If you do, it's probably a lie. You just need a plan. Maybe not a financial plan. Perhaps you need a life plan? A relationship plan? A plan for getting along better with your kids. It's not the plan that matters so much as the execution. Amazing things are revealed when we take a journey to reach our goals. Good luck on your journey whatever it may be.

Lessons Learned:

1) If you have a financial plan backed by an investment philosophy, you don't need a market outlook or to fear volatility.

2) Investing isn't a hobby. It's human nature to be emotional. Emotion reduces investment returns. We all think we can control our emotions when it comes to managing our own money. We can't. Stop lying to yourself.

3) Remember R.A.D. **R**ebalancing your portfolio at least yearly is immensely important. **A**sset allocation balances risk and reward. **D**iversification helps us reach our long-term financial goals. If we return to R.A.D. time and time again, we give ourselves the best chance of becoming successful investors.

Mindset Tips:

1) Anyone with the right mindset and a financial plan will be able to afford a meaningful and contented retirement.

2) One of the greatest abilities in investing is to develop patience as a mindset. The ability to do nothing and deliberately allow your plan the time it needs to work is difficult in times of market volitivity.

3) Embrace your uniqueness as a person and as an investor. Don't settle for an out of the box or cookie cutter financial plan. You deserve better.

Aha Moments and Self Reflections

Note your Thoughts

Jay Tsougrianis

Jay has a degree in management with a major in finance from the University of Calgary. She worked briefly selling mutual funds and as an analyst in the oil and gas industry before finding her way into pharmaceutical and medical sales. After years of pushing herself to the brink in order to be recognized, Jay suffered mental and physical burnout and left the industry.

After regaining her life balance, and re-evaluating her life purpose, she discovered that true joy came from helping others to become their best selves. She decided she wanted to help others through sharing what she had learned in her self-discovery journey and has since become a life coach with a focus on stress management, life balance, budgeting, and finance, as well as goal setting and accountability.

Jay now leads a public speaking club in Calgary, Alberta where she empowers others to speak their authentic truth and build their businesses through public speaking.

Connect with Jay:

Jay.mindovermatter@gmail.com

Chapter 8

Healing My Relationship with Money

By Jay Tsougrianis

"When things come easy, it's easy to lose sight of what really matters."
-Jay Tsougrianis, *Mind Over Matter Coaching*

Finding a job was easy, and sales come naturally to me. The best thing about sales is that you can earn more the more you sell. The bigger the carrot dangled in front of me the harder I worked, which earned me ever-increasing bonuses and led me to believe I deserved to have nice things. Besides, I had an image to uphold. I was one of the top sales reps in my company, and I had to look the part. Between my husband's income and my own, I believed we had it made. We quickly bought the big house, the nice cars, the vacation property, expensive clothes, beautiful furniture, you name it, we had it.

It's strange how things change, and now when I look back, I wonder what led me to value things so superficial? Why did I feel I needed to show off that we had great jobs with great incomes? Why did I feel the need to keep up with the Joneses? All of these things were supposed to make me happy. So why wasn't I happy, why did I always want more?

Forming My Relationship with Money

I grew up in a modest home on a farm outside of a small town in Saskatchewan. My father was a grain farmer, and my mother worked at the local bank and later at the nursing home or what we called, the old folks home. I had an amazing childhood, and I still have the fondest memories of growing up in a rural setting, where you could run in the streets, raid gardens and be invited into Mrs. Millar's home at Halloween to eat fresh cinnamon buns. Life in a small town was so different than living in the big city, and there are times I still dream of living that uncomplicated life once more.

When it came to money, I never knew how much money my parents earned, but I was very aware that they spent a lot of it on their children. If they weren't reminding us, other parents were sure to comment—often directly—to us kids or to my parents. They never understood why my folks spent their money on their kids, rather than traveling and partying with them. Lucky for us, they wanted to ensure we had every opportunity in school and sports, and so myself and my three older brothers were all well educated, and we were all good athletes. My dad made it very clear that he didn't want any of us to end up on the farm like he did and so he reinforced in all of us that secondary education was the only real way to earn a successful living.

My mother was well intending, and I knew she worked hard to earn a small salary in comparison to my father. She worked shift work with heavy lifting and still found the time and energy to get me the one hour drive to the city four nights a week to skate. She eventually suffered burnout and hired an older student to drive me to the city, so she could get healthy again. I know now that I never really understood the sacrifice she made when I was young. Looking back, and being a parent myself, I now realize just what my mother gave up for me.

On the long drives to the city to skate, my mother and I talked about money often. We didn't discuss how to make money or how to save money or budget, but rather how much everything cost. She wanted me to know that I was lucky to skate and that I had better appreciate the opportunity. Although it was important to my mom that I dressed in all the name brand clothes and had the nicest things, I grew up feeling guilty that all of this money "that does not grow on trees" was being spent on me. The worst part was that the dollars grew every time I was reminded. Something that cost $150 originally would somehow grow to $200 and then $250 the more I was reminded. With the increase in dollars, the increase in guilt multiplied.

I learned from my mother that my father was what one would call 'tight'. He never spent money on himself or my mother. They never went on holidays, and they didn't have a vacation home or timeshare like many of our friends. I understand now that although my father was supposedly tight, he would give the shirt off his back to make sure that his children, his siblings, and his parents were taken care of. He was generous in our small town and volunteered and donated often to ensure our town continued to grow and prosper.

My parents were obviously good with money, they never carried debt and taught us that if you can pay cash for something you pay cash. Credit cards are for emergency, and they must be paid off monthly. Most importantly, they taught us to work hard, show up on time and always give 100% at whatever job you have. Having a job is a privilege, and one should never take that for granted.

I found my first job in the summer between grade 10 and 11, working at a sporting goods store in Saskatoon. Since then, I've had all kinds of jobs, in all different areas (but that's another topic altogether). You see, my parents finally moved me to the city to live with my older brother, to room and board, when he wasn't around. Skating was everything, and they were willing to make sure I had the opportunity to go as far as I could. The expenses grew and now I was informed that it cost $25,000 a year to keep me on the ice. To be honest, I really didn't know how much money my parents earned at that point. Was it $50,000 or $150,000? In hindsight, I truly had no idea if this was a lot to them or a little.

To this day, I *still* have no idea. All I knew was this ever-increasing amount of money was being spent on me, and somehow there always seemed to be more (with a sprinkling of guilt of course.) At least now I was earning a little bit on my own, but like any teenager with their first job, I'm not exactly sure where that money went.

Although I was always very aware of how much everything cost, I never really understood why that mattered, because it seemed like I could have most anything I wanted. I grew up with the belief that if you earn money, you can buy things, and the more you earn, the more you can buy. Even after graduating with a degree in finance, I somehow ignored the fact that I had to spend less than I earned and that it was my responsibility to budget and save. Lucky for me, my parents supported me until I married a man who was much more responsible with his money than I had bothered to be with mine.

Just like my parents, no matter how much I spent, my husband was sure to take care of the bills. We seemed to always have money left over after investing, paying the bills and buying whatever we wanted. It was easy for me to carry on as I always had, knowing that someone would always take care of the 'money'. He would mention (okay, I'll be honest, we would argue) often that I needed to pay more attention to what came in and what went out, but I ignored his request to take responsibility. Why would I bother if he was doing it? He seemed to have everything under control. Our portfolio was growing nicely, and we really didn't carry any debt outside of our mortgage and the odd line of credit.

I know, right now you are probably thinking, *What in the hell can someone who has a mortgage like everyone else and no other debt teach me about money?* Well to be honest, a lot. You see, I had developed such a laissez-faire attitude to money that I ignored the fact that it was making me extremely unhappy. Chasing money to buy things does not make anybody happy. In fact, I've recently realized that all of these things that I had bought over the years have brought me nothing more than anxiety and guilt. You see, I *had* been listening to my husband when he said I needed to pay more attention to the finances, I had just pretended I didn't have time. Besides, I had a great job and had finally reached the income I had told myself was what you make when you are 'successful'. Little did I know at that earning that kind of money would be the unhappiest point of my life.

The Wake-Up Call

The longer I ignored my situation, the worse it got, especially when the economy slowed, and our paychecks were reduced. Deep down I knew I needed to reduce my spending, but I kept making the excuse that we had savings, and besides we "needed" the things I was buying. You know how it goes, this little ornament will make my home more welcoming, the new jeans I need because I'm working from home now, and let us not forget the $6.00 almond milk lattes for when I walk the dog. If you dig deep enough, you can make up an excuse to validate any purchase, and I had become an expert. At some point though you have to be honest with yourself and admit that savings aren't going to help you in the future if you continue to dip into them.

In 2017, I was introduced to Rule One Investing, otherwise known as the Warren Buffett style of value investing. I wasn't working anymore and I finally decided that I was going to stop fighting with my husband over money, and learn how to invest properly and be responsible for my own money. Yes, I know I said I have a degree in finance, but let's be honest, having book knowledge and knowing a bunch of formulas doesn't mean I actually trusted myself to invest my own money. Taking responsibility for my own investing has been challenging, but learning how to invest without making rash emotional decisions has been a catalyst for change in my entire life. Empowerment comes via responsibility after all, and understanding how much work it takes to make money in the market will definitely give you a wake-up call.

Cutting the Cord

After a year of not working at a full-time job, I was determined to find a way to stay at home and create a life that afforded me freedom from the corporate world. Unfortunately, when you are only working part-time the income that once afforded me to spend frivolously had all but disappeared. I had to find a way to build a sustainable business, while significantly reducing my expenses at the same time. This is where my journey truly began, and I had to do some serious soul searching. They say awareness is everything, and so I decided it was time I faced the truth.

A friend of mine suggested I watch a documentary called, *The Minimalists* by filmmakers Joshua Fields Millburn and Ryan Nicodemus. As I watched, it was as though a light bulb was finally turned on that exposed my spending for what it truly was, a facade to hide my true emotions. I started questioning the value of my things, my reasoning and the excuses I had used to justify my purchases, and why I had ignored the truth for so long. Was I using spending to fill a void? Could I even remember what I had bought even a few weeks earlier? What did I get for Christmas last year, what did I buy as gifts? It was all a blur, items purchased with little or no memory of why or what. These things that I spent our money on had brought momentary relief, but were not a long-term fix to make me happy and certainly not a way to move us closer to retirement. I quickly realized that these consumer items brought little to no joy to my life. These material possessions were just that, possessions, and they carried a heavy weight of guilt with them.

A few days later I decided to put myself to the test and find out what we were actually spending on and where all the money was going. I tediously pulled together every bank statement, the multiple credit card statements, lines of credits and mortgage statements, and sorted them into a multi-page spreadsheet. I categorized everything I could, from Starbucks, dining out, alcohol, groceries, insurance, mortgage, activities, travel, you name it, it had a category. When I finished and added it all up, it felt like I had been dragged across the hot coals of Hell. How had I been so naïve for so long? I was smart, I had a degree, I had held great jobs with high incomes and lots of responsibility. How then had I been so remiss about my own finances? What mental block did I have that pushed me so far away from the truth?

I had thought that by not building the big house like we had planned to do a few years earlier and moving into a small, more reasonable home was already all we needed to do. Besides, I had made a decision to quit drinking a year earlier, and I even stopped getting my nails done. Hadn't we had already significantly reduced our planned spend enough to make up for me not working full-time. I mean, our mortgage was already less than half of what we were planning a few years earlier. That, I realized, was the first and biggest lie I told myself. The second and probably most dangerous: that small spends don't add up to anything meaningful.

The Lies I Told Myself

1) But It Only Cost $5, $10, $20:

   You've heard it before, the latte factor, coined by David Bach. If we make our own coffee rather than buying it, we can invest the difference. Okay, that's a fair statement, but do any of us do it? I personally spent $2500 a year at Starbucks alone. Fast food and dining out for my family added up to a whopping $12,500, with 95% of those meals costing between $5 and $15. Did you read that? $15,000 a year because we didn't bother to make our own coffee or pack a lunch. If I had invested even half of that at 7%, I would have over $100,000 in ten years. Those almond lattes and cheap, unhealthy fast food better have tasted damn good.

2) It Was on Sale, and I Need It:

Oh, the power of advertising to make us believe we *need* to purchase all those things that will make our lives easier. You know exactly what I mean; the latest greatest iPhone with all those amazing app subscriptions, the luxury car with navigation, that new supplement that will help you lose weight, and hey it's fricken cold here, I *need* that Canada Goose Parka. In 2018 the average person saw 5000 advertisements per day. I don't know about you, but even people with amazingly strong willpower are going to be influenced by that amount of consumer advertising. These companies know exactly how to tap into our emotions and completely by-pass any rationality we think we have, and they are damn good at it.

3) It's Not My Fault; Nobody Taught Me:

I strongly believe that we are failing our children. Our education system is archaic and fails to address the life skills that we need in order to budget and invest responsibly. "Americans are dying with an average of $62,000 in debt" – CBS News. Budgeting should be considered a basic human skill and even though the average American has $38,000 in personal debt, we neglect to add this to our regular school curriculum. There are tools that are so advanced that all you need to do is enter a few numbers, the math is done for you, but if we have never been taught how to budget and our parents were never taught, the cycle will continue. So, guess what folks, it's up to us to invest in ourselves and learn to use the tools for ourselves.

4) But I Have a Great Salary:

This may be true, but at the end of the day, it is all relative. I've always wondered why when we apply for a job, we hang our hat on the gross salary? If you've ever gotten a paycheck, you know that we only see 50 to 60% after taxes, CPP, EI, etc. (Maybe slightly more if you have right-offs, but then there are other expenses you simply can't ignore.) We wear our salaries with pride, but neglect to be honest with ourselves that we don't earn anywhere near that much money. I'm pretty sure I'm not the only person who justified my spending with my gross salary rather than my net income.

5) I'm Still Young, What's the Rush

I used to work in an investment firm, and I was astonished by the number of people who would call me, who were already in their fifties and tell me they wanted to start investing so they could retire in ten years. Of course, my next question was always how much do you have saved already and how much do you need to have to retire? More often than not the answer was under $10,000 in savings, and they needed well over $50,000 a year to live. Yes, you read that right. How have we failed our citizens so badly that even grown adults don't understand compounding and retirement planning? No matter how young or old you already are, you need a retirement plan (and if not you, your spouse).

Managing your money doesn't have to be scary. As my coaching instructor, Kain Ramsay always says, "Empowerment comes via responsibility." Once you take responsibility for your own finances you will find yourself feeling more empowered day by day. When I first started, it seemed overwhelming, but now saying no to wasting money has become second nature. Challenge your thoughts, challenge your wants and learn to walk away. Keep a list of the things you think you need, and if you still need it in thirty days, then go back and make the purchase. You will almost always find that the desire will go away, and you may even forget why you thought you needed it in the first place. So, take control, and if you need help, I am always here to help you on your journey to a balanced budget.

Lessons Learned:

1) Educate yourself and your children; it is your responsibility to learn how to budget and how to invest. If you need help, find a knowledgeable mentor, coach, advisor or friend who can help you. The internet can be your best friend with hundreds of free videos and blogs on the subject (just be sure not to buy into any courses or quick get rich schemes because of good marketing).

2) Be in the know; build yourself a spreadsheet with all your spending for the last year. Your bank statements are all available online, so there is no excuse. Be honest with your categories and test yourself to see if you actually remember what you purchased and whether it still something you truly believe you had to have.

3) Constantly question your thoughts, motivation, desires, and biases when you are about to make a purchase. Why do I need this? Will this purchase add value to my life? Will buying this get me to where I want to go? Will I feel guilty if I buy this? Am I looking at all the evidence or just what supports my desire in this moment? Am I making this purchase out of habit?

Mindset Tips:

1) Be gentle with yourself. The past is the past, and all you can do is learn from it and move forward. View your mistakes as opportunities you can learn from. Allow yourself to be uncomfortable, as this is when you will have the biggest breakthroughs.

2) You can do this; it's never too late. Every step forward you make is one step ahead of yesterday. Getting started will build momentum and managing your money will become second nature if you practice.

3) Be grateful for all that you will learn and how much you will grow as you go through this journey to become financially empowered.

Aha Moments and Self Reflections

Note your Thoughts

Hong Wang

Hong was born and raised in China, she studied philosophy in Jilin University in China, worked as a teacher in Shenyang University for seven years, and immigrated to Canada in 1993. She currently lives in Calgary.

Hong retrained herself to be a computer programmer and worked in downtown, then quickly decided to become a stay-at-home mom. As her children grew, she ventured into a self-employment career, starting with a multi-level marketing company; then became a license RESP sales representative, and finally a license realtor in province of Alberta.

Hong is very enthusiastic about her work in the real estate industry, she loves to help her clients buy or sell their home, and especially enjoys advising new immigrants and real estate investors. She volunteers regally at the Calgary Real Estate Board, as well as charities in the city and the Chinese community. When not busy at work, Hong enjoys the great outdoors in and around the city, and Salsa dancing.

Connect with Hong:

HongTheRealtor@gmail.com

Chapter 9

The Choices We Make

By Hong Wang

I was born and raised in the city of Shenyang in the northeast part of China. I came to Canada when I was twenty-eight years old to join my husband.

A Career Woman

I came to Ottawa in the summer of 1993. The air was warm and fresh; people wore shorts and sandals, and everybody was enjoying the summer. I remembered strolling around after touring the Parliament Hills for the first time, looking at the huge maple leaf flag dancing in the wind, with my heart full of happiness and excitement.

I knew very well that starting a new life in a new country wouldn't be easy, so I enrolled in an ESL school right away. The lady sitting behind the desk at the ESL school was super friendly, like everyone I had met in this country. As well as giving me the basic information, she asked me if we had children. She said, "You can have a baby now. Even if you don't have a job, the government will help you raise your baby." Her beautiful blue eyes were full of compassion when she spoke. I said my priority was to find a job, to "find a place in this society for myself." She gave a big smile, turned to my husband and said, "Your wife is a career woman."

My journey of being a career woman took longer than I thought. My son was born one day before the first anniversary coming to Canada, by C-section. My husband was working for the National Library on a contract, and he did not take one day off work. I spent three days in the hospital and took care of my son on my own afterward. Three years later, my mother-in-law visited us and stayed for nine months, so I started working part-time and going to school again. The economy was slow in Ontario at the time, but there were a lot of jobs in IT. While taking more ESL classes at the Algonquin College, I made friends with a girl who also came from China a few years earlier. We took an aptitude exam together, and to everybody's surprise, I passed. After a couple of rounds of interviews, I was accepted into a special program that was created by (back then) the Revenue Canada to train programmers fixing the legacy code in order to avoid Y2K problems. It was a great opportunity. The program had twenty spaces, but they were only able to find eighteen people. Everyone who graduated from the program would be working for Revenue Canada, but I ended up not going because, at the same time, my husband got a very good job offer in Toronto. He was very excited because his salary was doubled. So, without even setting foot in Toronto before, we moved to the 'center of the universe'.

We lived in Toronto for a year. I completed an Application Programming certificate in what was then known as Ryerson Polytechnic through part-time study, but I disliked living in the big city very much. I grew up in a multi-million population city in China, so I never thought I would feel that way. Raising a three-year-old boy in a forest of concrete was very stressful, and buying a home seemed to be impossible, given our first-time buyer's budget and the size of the city. My husband was sent to work for a project in Calgary where the company's head office was located for a few months. The very first night he called me, he said that China Town in Calgary was the cleanest he had ever seen in U.S. and Canada. Also, housing prices were so low compared with Toronto—which still is true today, more than twenty years later. I took my son for a short visit, and we immediately fell in love with the 'small' city. We visited the show homes that were featured in the Calgary Herald that weekend. I was pleasantly surprised that we could afford to buy a brand-new house only half an hour away from downtown for less than what we could get for a high-rise condo in some satellite cities in Toronto. The house also included a front yard *and* a back yard. My husband put in a request to transfer, and after much negotiation, we moved to Calgary. I still remember the day we left Toronto. It was the end of June, at 5 a.m. and it was already 30 degrees Celsius. The air was so humid I found it hard to breathe. When we settled down in the apartment in Calgary that afternoon, I threw myself in bed, listened to the leaves rustling outside the window, and I sighed. It was heaven.

Again, I enrolled myself in school. This time it was the SAIT, The Southern Alberta Institute of Technology, in a program that came with a practicum term. I found a small software company in downtown to do the practicum and stayed working after graduation. It was spring 1999, six years after I first came to Canada. So it appeared that I finally found my place in my new home. IT was a good field to be in. I enjoyed the work, and the salary was great for beginners.

My husband traveled a lot for work, so most of the time I was home alone with my young son. I didn't drive at the time, and I found out very quickly that the life of a working professional woman with a small child was very stressful. Every day we left the house before seven so I could drop him off at the daycare, hop on a bus to get to the train, and walk a few blocks to work; I would see my son again before 6 pm, just before the daycare closed; and by 8:30 p.m. he would have to be in bed. It was always a struggle to get my son out of bed in the morning. He would say, "Mom, but I am still tired." I would say, "Maybe you can take a nap at daycare later." I then found myself saying, "I don't care, you need to get up *now*." when he was still in bed after a few calls. On top of that, I quickly found out how often little children at daycare got sick, and that I would have to miss work and stay home with him.

For months afterward, when I was sitting in the morning bus, filled with the mixture of scents from everybody's perfume, shampoo, deodorant and sometimes breakfast, I wondered, *Why am I leaving my child to other people's care and going to work for someone?* While I was lying in bed remembering the heartache from missing my parents so many years ago, I wondered just how much better my son was having it. We were a 'cell' family of three— there were no grandmothers, no aunts or uncles, no cousins. I was all he had, and he saw me awake for no more than three hours a day.

My son started school the following year. School time is 9 a.m. to 3 p.m. in Canada. Just when I thought leaving my son at daycare all day long was hard enough, now I was in a thicker jam. The school my son was going to didn't offer any before or after school care. The only child care I could find was a day home, but they had cats, and my son was very allergic. By this time, I started to think that China had it right. Any sizable employers, being a factory, a government organization, the college I worked at, all had their own childcare center. Little children would go with their parents to work, and they would come home together after work, unless of course, in my case, my childcare center was considered superb to have the older children stay for a whole week. I was miserable, but the parents all thought they were so lucky. I started to believe the system in Canada was a 'conspiracy' set up against working mothers.

My son was going to a charter school for gifted children located in one of the many small buildings of an old military base. There was a small software company in the next building, and one of my friends knew someone who worked there. Miraculously, I was able to get a job there. By this time, I had learned how to drive, and I negotiated working hours from 9 a.m. to 3 p.m. This job didn't last very long, by the end of the year, the dot-com bubble burst, NASDAQ lost seventy-five percent of its value, and both small companies I worked for were wiped out. I was laid off, but not surprisingly, I didn't take it very hard. I felt like I had gone up to the mountain and come down. I was convinced that for the time being, my most valuable contribution to the world was being a mother to my son. Everybody could be a programmer, but I am the only mother he had, and I had to be the best I could be. Raising a happy and confident child is the most valuable and important work a mother can do.

When my best friend from SAIT found out I was not going to look for a job again, he said, "That's a pity; you are such a good programmer. What a waste." I beamed at him and said, "I am going to waste all my intellect on raising my son so he will not know the pain of missing his mom."

At the end of 2001, I gave birth to my daughter. I immersed myself into motherhood, and I did everything a stay-at-home mom would do with her baby: we went to playgroups, the library, the zoo, swimming, and dancing. We played outside all the time. We went to see her big brother at all his school concerts, assemblies, and sports days. When my daughter started school, I would volunteer all the time for reading, hot lunches, and field trips. I was always there, and I knew she was so proud of me.

Real Estate—Where Family and Career Meet

Back when I was working, it didn't take long till I figured that there wasn't much left of my junior programmer's salary after paying taxes, childcare, and gas. It would be many years later that I learned the term 'tax freedom day'. If the average Canadian pays all their taxes up front, they would have to pay all the money they make till this day to all levels of governments. It is generally sometime in June. For example, tax freedom day was June 7th in 2016, June 9th in 2017, and June 10th in 2018.

I thought to myself, *There must be better ways to make more and keep more money*. After all, this is a capitalist country. However, 'the evil' of working full-time is that I had no time nor energy to think and explore anything on that matter. Without a job, I was reading all the books I could find about money and personal finance. I found a whole new world of knowledge about self-employment, family business, and entrepreneurship. I learned that many people with MBA degrees didn't make more than immigrants who bought a small business. That a dry-cleaning store was one of the most profitable businesses. I also learned that investing in real estate was a really good idea because, you can leverage your purchase power through mortgage. If you are educated, you can get a rental property and have the rent cover all the expenses, and by the time the mortgage is paid off, the value of the house would have doubled.

I knew that I was fortunate to be able to quit working because my husband's salary was good enough for us to live a moderate life. I also felt that even though—like all stay-at-home moms—I worked much harder at home and saved hundreds of thousands in expenses, (therefore making a financial contribution to the family indirectly), I still didn't feel completely accomplished because I was not bringing home a paycheck. All this reading opened my mind. I realized that I could do things I never knew existed. I didn't have to be a career woman to realize my value, and what was a 'career' after all? It didn't have to be going to a job downtown. I was brought up to be a good student and a good employee. I was a college teacher; I was a programmer; I had never had the aspiration to be an entrepreneur, but I could start now? Who said I couldn't?

I was very excited and encouraged by this new-found knowledge. I followed suggestions from some books and joined a multi-level marketing company that sold educational toys and books. I have to say, there had never been any businessmen in generations of my immediate or extended families. I had never taken any sales or marketing training, and the sheer idea of selling was frightening. One of the obvious benefits of any multi-level marketing was the training, not only on product lines, but more importantly the business mindset and networking with people. For two years, I tried my best to share and discuss my toys and books with like-minded mothers. I was never very good at recruiting, which seemed to be more important, but I was just happy that all the cool toys were paid by my commission and, on top of that, I did make some money and made lots of new friends.

We had Registered Education Saving Plans (RESPs), for both of my kids within months of their births. With my son, the options were limited to a few RESP group trust fund providers. By the time my daughter was born, you could get RESP set up at banks, just like RRSPs. So, my son's RESP was a group plan, and my daughter's was a mutual fund account at a bank.

One day, when my daughter was three, both of my children's RESP statements came in the mail. My son's plan had a government-imposed mandate that insured the principle would never be lost and had shown significant growth every year even though their investment objective was conservative. My daughter's, on the other hand, were a few mutual funds picked out based on a risk assessment. Not only did the fund not make any money, but had lost about twenty percent of the principal contribution within three years. I picked up the phone and called the sales rep whose name and phone number were printed on my son's statement. Within hours, Don, the sales rep, came to my house. When he pulled over in front of my house and got out of his bright red jeep wearing a bright yellow fleece pull-over hoodie, I was watching my daughter playing in the front yard. The first thing I said to him was, "I think I can do what you are doing."

Don was a retired high school principal. He owned a sales branch of the RESP distribution company, he started the business because he got "bored of retirement." He was a very lovely gentleman with a great sense of humor. He said his color choices were his way of dealing with his middle-age crisis. I worked at Don's branch for four years as a licensed sales rep and it was a great time. I was getting more and more comfortable talking about the product with new parents, and I felt very proud that I could bring a great option to them that their children will benefit hugely in years to come. The sales rep job was completely commission-based and had completely flexible working hours, it worked out great for me. I would be with my little girl during the day, making dinner before my son go off school. I made business phone calls whenever I could, and met my clients at their homes during evenings and weekends. My first year's commission total was more than my programmer's salary, and because I could deduct lots of expenses, I paid less tax.

Looking back on how I had struggled and tried to figure out how to choose between family and career, I wish someone had told me that I didn't have to worry; that all was going to work out. As long as I follow my heart and do the most important things, things will always work out.

We lived in our first home for seven years. In winter 2004, we sold it for just over $200,000 and moved into a bigger home in the same community the following spring. Alberta's economy had a very good couple of years, thanks to the rising oil price, and by the end of 2006, housing prices doubled.

It was a perfect time for amateur investors like us to get into real estate investment. The value of our home went up and up, we were able to take money out as a home equity line of credit (HELC), and use it for down payment. The lending rules were so much more favorable for buyers so getting a mortgage was quite easy. During these couple of years, we bought a few rental properties.

In 2008, I obtained both my real estate and life insurance licenses, I decided to focus on real estate shortly after.

I have always envied those who knew exactly what they wanted to do from a young age. I was never crystal clear on what I wanted to be when I grew up. Becoming a realtor was not my childhood aspiration. When I left China, there was not even such a word as 'realtor' in Chinese vocabulary. It seemed I just did what made the most sense to me at that moment, and I listened to my heart at important times. Now I get to work with families buying or selling their home, their biggest asset, their most precious belonging, and I get to take care of my own children while doing it. I am taking care of two families at the same time always, it feels great!

Fifty - Fifty

"One shall be established at the age of thirty, be unfazed at the age of forty, and know your fate at age fifty."
- Lao Zi

The year before I turned fifty, I started to feel a sense of urgency. I realized that if I didn't start doing some of the things I wanted to do "someday", those items on my 'bucket list', I might never get to do them. I started to pay a lot of attention to how I spent my time, I was very focused on business and worked very hard. I guess that was what a mid-life crisis felt like.

Meanwhile, my husband spent ten months in China to be with my mother-in-law, who fell ill and eventually passed away. He was also laid off by the company he worked for seventeen years because he simply didn't return to work after his vacation time was all used up. He turned fifty that year.

None of us felt terribly bad about him being laid off, as he worked hard enough for long enough at the job. We had worked on our rental properties, went to real estate investment events for years and we had lots of ideas about how to bring that up to the next level. We agreed he should just take some time off, to grieve his mother's passing, to recover physically, and to figure out what to do next. However, three months later, I found out he was having an affair. On my fiftieth birthday, I took off my wedding ring. A couple of months later, exactly one year after he came back from China, I asked him to move out. To be betrayed by my husband was the hardest blow I had in my life.

Then came one of the most unpleasant parts of divorce: dividing the assets.

When we came to Canada, we had nothing. Everything we owned were assets accumulated during marriage. According to Canadian law, everything would be split between him and me 50/50. Personally, I think it is ridiculously unfair as the law didn't see the children being the ones needing the money most, especially young children. The law is very focused on custody and parenting, but when it comes to the money, children are invisible.

The RESPs seemed to be a better idea, even though at the time, none of us had a sliver of idea that one day this money would be all they had under their name. It pained me so bad. If I could go back in time, I would start a trust for each of my kids the day they were born. I would make them an equal owner of everything we had: every investment and every real estate property. I would make my husband sign a contract saying that if we get divorced, we would split all assets with the kids. I am sure this can be done. I believe this should be a part of every family's financial planning. If a couple cannot do this, they are not strong enough to have children.

One of the few things I learned from my philosophy study is the belief that everything happens for a reason, and the right choice is never the easy one. I can't tell you how many times I had woke up in the dark of the night thinking, *I am a divorced woman now.* Losing my marriage was sad, but I also felt liberated. I know there were many women who stay in their marriages because of financial reasons, because they sacrificed their career to raise their families and believed they are not employable anymore. I am glad I can make the choices I want. I learned that following my heart had never failed me. For me, that's what "knowing your fate" really means.

Lessons Learned:

1) Follow your heart, and the money will follow you. Women will forever face the challenge of juggling a career and family. Do what's best for you, and trust that the rest will follow.

2) Hope for the best, prepare for the worst. According to the latest Statistics Canada data (Nov 2018), about thirty-eight percent of all marriages end in divorce. Getting a separation agreement ready at the time of getting married is a good idea, it might even save your marriage.

3) Obstacles are the wrong side of opportunity; it'll be clear as day when you overcome it and look back.

Mindset Tips:

1) Being rich is our birthright, we all deserve to live comfortably, have fine things to enjoy, and have our mind and spirit enriched. Seeking and growing wealth is part of the law of the universe, all living things have only one fundamental purpose, that is to expand, to be better, stronger and bigger.

2) Have a clear vision of your why. Inject emotion in it. Bring yourself to it whenever you feel down, disappointed and defeated.

3) Always be grateful, because we truly are privileged by just living in this great country.

Aha Moments and Self Reflections

Note your Thoughts

Jenn Widney

Ever wonder what it would be like to live debt free? After robbing her daughter's piggy bank to pay a credit card bill that she couldn't afford, Jenn Widney remembers thinking, *This cannot be my life. How did I get here?*

Jenn became mortgage free at the age of thirty-three, and her experience has fueled a passion for helping people achieve financial freedom and release themselves from the burden of debt. She is a Ramsey Solutions Financial Coach Master Trainer and has her BA in Psychology from the University of Calgary. She loves to make finances interesting and fun, and cash flow plans are her superpower.

Connect with Jenn:

FinancialFun.Gals@gmail.com

Chapter 10

Relationship Rescue: Cash Flow 911

By Jenn Widney

As a kid, instead of playing house, I played bank. I liked numbers and could play bank for hours. My bank was funded with Monopoly money and I'm pretty confident the customers enjoyed the short lines and five-hundred-dollar bills. The make-believe was even more fun when my mom would let me bring a few blank deposit and withdrawal slips home from the real bank. Remember when we used to use paper at the bank? My heart almost exploded with excitement when my mom changed accounts and let me have her old unused checks to play with. When I wasn't playing bank, the moment my friends were interested, I would quickly pull out the actual Monopoly game and beg to be the banker.

You would think my inherent interest in numbers and money meant finances came easily. Nothing could be further from the truth. I didn't know terrifying financial dangers were lurking in the real world. My innocent fake bank only dealt in deposits and withdrawals...not credit.

I grew up in a house where money was a grown up topic. My sister and I always had what we needed, but my parents never brought us into the money conversation. I'm not saying this is bad or good. We just carried on with life while money happened behind the scenes. I felt reassured knowing everything was always taken care of, but I believe I could have handled knowing some of the responsibility of how money works in 'grown up' life.

As a kid, I knew my parents were the best. Everyone wanted to play and hang out at our house. Besides having stationary from a real bank, my mom had the best snacks, and my dad was hilarious, always telling jokes and playing pranks. From a child's perspective, the best part about our house was the lack of a limit on how many friends were allowed to stop by after school. Now as an adult, I understand that my parents weren't only the best; they were complete *geniuses*. The best way to know your kids aren't getting into any trouble is to have them at home with you. Well played, Mom and Dad.

I am forever grateful to my parents for all of the opportunities I've had because of what I learned from them and the way I was raised. One of my earliest childhood money memories was going shopping with my mom before Christmas to pick out a toy to donate. Have you ever looked at toys knowing something you choose could possibly be a child's *only* gift? The enormity of this reality was not lost on me.

Other than learning to be generous and kind to others, both with my time and finances, there were no lessons on money. Which, to be fair, is not uncommon. I rarely encounter an adult who raves about the intentional financial teachings they learned growing up. Can you think of someone who raves about their financial upbringing? Me either. Instead, our parents do the best they can to take care of all of life's responsibilities. We just pick up what we can, watching from afar. Sometimes parents, for whatever reason, don't do a great job handling life's responsibilities. Kids learn from that experience too.

Once you're an adult, our society assumes you should understand money. But with no intentional financial education, how are you to know? Sort of like when you have your first child. Suddenly you're a parent, and you realize you know zero about keeping another human being alive or how to raise them into a contributing, responsible member of society. Bills show up, and you pay them. You confidently tell yourself, *Okay, I can do that.*

Then a credit card offer comes your way, and you naively think, *I've heard a credit card builds my credit score. Better get one of those to prove I'm a responsible adult who makes good money decisions.* Sound familiar?

Applying for my first credit card felt like a rite of passage to maturity. I had done it without my parents' permission or signature. When the card came in the mail with my name on it, I felt like a huge life milestone was reached. Something about it felt as if the universe was saying, "Welcome to adulthood, Jenn. You are now capable of all sorts of amazing financial decisions. You have a credit card at your fingertips, which *only responsible* adults are trusted with." I was clearly ready to conquer the world with my credit card responsibly by my side.

I was positive I had a failsafe plan ready to go. My *intention* was to use my credit card *only* for necessities, and pay it off immediately each month. I didn't want to carry a balance and pay interest. My noble purpose was to build this mysterious credit score everyone seemed to rave was so important.

It will come as no surprise that my failsafe plan failed. Swiping the credit card became more and more common as the weeks and months passed. Making immediate payments grew old quickly. I became desperate to maintain my need to be a responsible adult and turned to rationalization. Because I'm very creative and persuasive, I justified how pretty much anything I wanted was a necessity.

Fast forward a few years, and the immaturity of my questionable financial choices became quite clear when my spouse lost his job weeks after I had gone back to school. Suddenly, our income was gone. We had no warning it would happen, certainly didn't plan ahead with savings. Somehow, we had managed to keep our heads above water until then. I honestly thought we were expert money managers. A job loss, combined with unwise financial habits like use of credit, no cash flow plan, and no savings quickly snowballed into bills we couldn't pay and the realization we had no idea what we were doing.

Our lack of money and limited financial knowledge created crippling stress. The bills kept coming, and we did very little to change our spending habits, mainly because we didn't know how. My shiny credit card had been the recipe for our financial disaster.

Rock bottom for me was sneaking into my daughter's room to empty her piggy bank. It was a desperate attempt to pull together enough money to pay a credit card bill. Humiliated barely scratches the surface on how devastated I felt to steal from a baby, simply to cover up my financial mistakes.

We now found ourselves feeling alone, embarrassed, and unsure of what to do next. Should we ask our parents for money? Do we need to sell our house? Would a line of credit help? How long can we carry on before we lose everything?

In these types of situations, when people get into debt, banks offer math-based solutions like consolidation loans. In theory, a consolidation loan is mathematically sound. Put together high interest debts and combine them into one easy monthly payment at a lower interest rate. The assumption is more debt will not be accumulated, and payments will continue until the loan is paid off. But the debt is still there; it just gets moved and restructured. One payment would not financially educate us any more than when we first got into debt. How on earth could this help us avoid getting into debt again, and again, and *again*? It did not feel like a solution to us. It felt like a band-aid fix for something that needed a surgical overhaul. What would heal this crippling situation? And what about the *human* that racked up the debt in the first place?

I've come to believe consolidation loans are like offering transfusions to people hemorrhaging blood, without closing the wound. We've addressed the symptom of bleeding but not the problem of the open wound. We *need* to stop the bleeding (spending) if they have any chance of surviving (freedom from debt).

My husband and I weren't financially healthy. We knew our consumer debts weren't the only issue in need of attention. How we interacted with money and our relationship to it needed help too, and the bank didn't have the right solution for us.

Over the upcoming weeks and months, we started to factor the *human* side of money into our financial equation. Tackling our debt was so much more than the numbers. It was learning how to successfully navigate our relationship with money. We needed to learn sound financial habits to take us in the right direction.

We wanted to feel confident in our financial decision making and secure in case of an emergency. We believed working together would strengthen our marriage. We asked, "What are the emotions we attached to money, as individuals and a couple?" Unpacking what each money decision *felt* like was imperative to our journey in order to build a healthy relationship with our finances.

In order for my husband and I to get out of debt, we became active participants in our relationship with money instead of passive observers along for the not-always-pleasant ride. To become an active participant meant being intentional with our spending. To achieve that, we needed to be very clear about what we valued most in our life. Then we needed to ask ourselves, "Is our spending in line with those values?"

Answering that question sucked. We felt disappointed sifting through the financial wreckage. What we claimed to value most had been put to the side, instead of used to guide our financial choices.

I had been telling myself that above all else, I valued *time* with my family. But in asking the hard questions, I realized that constantly spending money on the *little extras* for our kids was *way* out of line with that value. The extra purchases meant more *time away* from my family to earn extra income to pay for the items. I've found that children just want to be with you. Most items are quickly discarded, and the empty cardboard box or a fun game of tag around the house is what children prefer.

Another realization was saying I value my *relationship* with my husband. But then I would hide purchases I didn't want him to know about. That deception caused me to be dishonest with him and myself. I claimed to value a better relationship with my husband, but my interaction with money didn't show it. Looking back, I've realized the financial decisions I made were actually eroding the quality of our relationship, one purchase at a time.

My spending was not in line with my time and relationship values. Furthermore, what I valued had *nothing* to do with money.

Over the years I have learned that identifying your values is extremely important to develop a successful financial plan. The numbers typically fall in line a little easier once you know what's important to you. Revisiting those values allow you to restructure spending habits to include human interaction with the money.

I find that when you align your values, *what* you care about most, with *how* you spend money, paying off debt doesn't become a chore. Because it's important, you make it a *choice*. You don't have to cut out what you love and sacrifice joy. You choose to say yes to being debt free and spend based on your values.

As my husband and I set out to live a life free from consumer debt, we created systems that allowed our values to guide our financial decisions. Together we developed cash flow plans and financial goals. It became a relationship building process.

We continue to use those plans and strategies to move through our daily financial decisions. Having a financial foundation built on our values allows us to move more smoothly through money conversations. When we encounter a roadblock, we work together to uncover what value is out of alignment that causes the financial challenge or disagreement.

Second only to cash flow planning, financial goal setting continues to be one of the best practices we have introduced to our relationship. When we set financial goals, we experience a deeper level of intimacy by sharing our hopes and dreams for the future. Our first big financial goal was to become debt free. This goal became the driving force behind all of our cash flow planning decisions. Having a target to work towards kept us focused on our 'yes' to being debt free. Our goals are now broken into short-term, like family vacations, and long-term savings for retirement.

Now I want to take a moment to let you focus on your financial situation. Take a minute to identify three things you are most grateful for in your life. What is it you cannot imagine living without? Write it on a piece of paper or in this book, as we will come back to these answers in the next step. As you can probably guess, the answer I hear most often to this question is rarely a material object. Rather, they tell me something like, "I'm grateful for my family, health, and friends."

What if you value health, but your relationship with money involves stress and anxiety? That certainly isn't in alignment with living a life of gratitude and valuing health. Or you borrow money from a family member, but you claim to be grateful for family, and now there is a huge strain on the relationship? In both of these scenarios, you need to re-evaluate your spending decisions and modify them to be consistent with your values rather than being in competition with them.

The most efficient and effective way to get your spending in line with the values you have identified is a cash flow plan, also known as a budget. A cash flow plan is where you map out how you will spend your money. My husband and I create a new cash flow plan at the *beginning* of every single month. This is our opportunity to assign each dollar of income to an expense or savings job. Some dollars go to expenses like utility payments and gas money. Others to fun expenses like entertainment and travel. Some may be assigned to saving while others to debt repayment. What is most important about your cash flow plan is that your expenses do not exceed your income, and every single dollar is assigned a job. This does *not* mean that every dollar needs to be spent. As I mentioned, some money should be assigned to savings.

The point of this exercise is to know where all your money is going instead of wondering where it went. If expenses are more than income, your choices are to increase income, decrease expenses, or a combination of both. I hope by reading about my experience, you understand the danger of not using a cash flow plan and instead relying on a credit card to live beyond your income. From the bottom of my heart, it was not a fun experience. I have yet to meet someone who says, "Jenn, I sure love consumer debt. It's so relaxing owing money and wondering how I'm going to pay my bills next month."

The cash flow plan is both the road map to spending in alignment with your values and the vehicle to reach your future financial goals. Now you might be thinking, *I said I valued my family, my health, and my home. Many of my dollars go to property taxes and house insurance…where does that fit?* If you are someone that values home ownership, there are some financial obligations that come with this luxury. You also want to be sure that the expense doesn't take more than its fair share of your dollars. Now that we're mortgage free, this amount is barely five percent of our income. When we had a mortgage, we worked hard to keep this number around twenty-five percent.

When you create a cash flow plan, be mindful that you are an active participant in your financial decisions. For example, I choose to have the financial security of life insurance, which means I choose to have it as a line item on my cash flow plan. I choose to have a cell phone, which means I choose to assign some of my dollars to that expense. On the other hand, I choose to bank where there are no banking fees because I do not want to allocate those costs on my cash flow plan.

If you are in a relationship, a monthly cash flow plan is a great opportunity to develop open communication with your partner about a topic that can create conflict for many couples. Share what your financial needs and goals are, and be open to hear and support their needs and goals as well. Never use a cash flow plan as a weapon to control your partner. The human side of money is complex, and your partner will have their own experiences with money to bring to the relationship. You will have differences, and that's okay. Work through them, and get outside help if necessary. Communication is key. When there is a challenge, ask questions and seek to understand.

Remember I said the cash flow plan helps you get closer to your financial goals? While a monthly plan is a great way to manage your day-to-day and month-to-month spending, you still need to account for annual and lifetime goals. At the beginning of the year, my husband and I always revisit our big future goals. Are we on track, and are there any necessary adjustments? Before we assign one single dollar to spend, we have a predetermined percentage of our dollars assigned to take care of our future. These dollars are put aside in investments for when we are ready to retire. This financial habit is extremely important because it helps determine the quality of our lives in the future. If you're young, it might not be sexy or fun to save money you probably won't need for years, but I believe it's better than the alternative. Don't get to that stage of life and not have any money to take care of yourself. If you are closer to needing the 'future you' money, cash flow planning is even more important to make the best use of the dollars you have saved.

Cash flow plans have a bad reputation as being restrictive... especially when they go by their other name... the B word... *budget*. I choose to see them from the opposite perspective. I believe my cash flow plan, aka *budget*, is the key to unlock my financial goals and ultimately lead to financial freedom. While there are occasions that require me to say *no* to gratifying an immediate want, it is solely for the purpose to say *yes* to future goals and desires. Each financial decision I make, no matter how small, is from a perspective of opportunity. I am grateful for the life I have, and the daily decisions I continue to make ensure I will be grateful for the future life I create.

I am passionate about empowering others to live financially free from the burden of consumer debt. I hope you have seen through my story that both positive and negative financial experiences create opportunities for us to learn and move in a healthier direction. My company, Financial Fundamentals, is built on a foundation of sound financial concepts and common sense. I believe financial literacy needs to be accessible and simplified for everyone to understand. Our culture has over-complicated an otherwise straightforward topic to the point that many people feel like they can "never win" with money. Like the game of Monopoly, their life is one of, "Do not pass go. Do not collect $200. Go directly to jail."

We fail our children when we bring them up into a culture that believes in instant gratification rather than saving for a rainy day. I want my children to know there are no limits and no boundaries to their potential. They can be and do anything they want to with their life. And I want them to grow up knowing never to spend the whole dollar and to become familiar with the boundaries and choices of spending within their means.

I encourage you to step into the financial future you desire. Become friends with your cash flow plans. A healthy relationship with money will lead to your financial goals and financial freedom.

Lessons Learned:

1) Tackling debt is so much more than the numbers. It is learning how to successfully navigate your relationship with money.

2) Identifying your values is extremely important to develop a successful financial plan.

3) The most efficient and effective way to get your spending in alignment with your values is a cash flow plan designed to bring you closer to your financial goals.

Mindset Tips:

1) Take an active role in your money choices by imagining yourself in the driver's seat of your financial decisions.

2) Let your values in life guide your spending. This will create a deeper sense of abundance.

3) Using your cash flow plan effectively is the key to unlocking your financial goals. Becoming best friends with my cash flow plans is one of the best things I have ever done for my finances.

Aha Moments and Self Reflections

Note your Thoughts

Heather Andrews

Visibility strategist, publisher, and 6x international bestselling author, Heather Andrews helps her clients share their story with the world by publishing their works online and offline. Heather believes we all have a story to share to help inspire other by publishing their works in books and podcasts.

With her publishing company, and podcast agency, Tenacious Living, she has published over 80 authors in one year and interviewed over 60 individuals to be seen and heard with the power of their story.

As a speaker, Heather inspires audiences by sharing her challenges and the survival strategies that continue to help her optimize adversity. Being a voice in self-discovery and revitalization, she is making a positive difference. She believes in the power of reinvention and helps inspire others to do the same.

Connect with Heather:

Heatherandrews.press

Followitthrupublishing.com

Chapter 11

Learning in the Debt

By Heather Andrews

I stood there in front of the pump, plagued with anxiety as I punched in my PIN number. I closed my eyes for a split second and said a silent micro-prayer. APPROVED appeared on the LED display. My breath rose up around me like a storm cloud in the cold morning air, as I audibly exhaled.

That day, standing at the gas station and praying for my gas purchase to go through on my credit card—I knew things *had* to change. And fast. You see it was not always this way.

They say there is good debt and bad debt. The jury is still out on this topic. All I know for sure is that I never used to have debt and now I do, a mountain of it. However, what I've learned through this entrepreneurial journey I'm on, is there are undeniably *good investments* and *bad investments*.

Let me tell you more…

I was at the rock bottom of my financial story. I was blessed enough to meet a woman who taught a class called Debt Destruction. On the first day of class, the teacher said, "Money should be a simple! It is numbers and if you don't have the money, you don't spend it."

If only it were that easy. Unfortunately, there is the human aspect of money and most of the world falls into this space—the space where life happens whether we are financially prepared, or not.

As a human, I feel this is where my relationship with money began. Growing up, my amazing mom drove a school bus. She loved the kids she took to and from school each day. My dad was an entrepreneur who built a six-figure revenue company serving rural farming communities from 1970 to 1997. I was blessed to grow up in a family where I really wanted for nothing. My dad took care of our day-to-day living and our future, while mom's income covered the 'extras.' My dad had a strong work ethic. Long hours, believing in something more, and going the extra mile to serve people was his motto. I am happy I fished these traits out of the gene pool! Granted there were hard times when the recession hit in the '80s, but my mom and dad were always open about where they stood financially.

I was baby-sitting by age twelve, working part-time by fourteen and have not stopped since. I started my healthcare career when I was twenty. I have worked all over the world and my career has been financially successfully. Healthcare was rewarding, but after a number of years I needed something more; almost like a 'happy place' to escape to. Healthcare can be an emotionally difficult vocation, when you're always seeing people at their worst even, though you are giving them your best.

I was enamored with a clothing line produced by a Canadian fashion designer, distributed through a network marketing business model. I signed up after the birth of my third child. I needed to do something different emotionally. It also allowed me to go part-time at work.

I moved up the sales chain very quickly, achieving top rank of new sales person across Canada. I loved the inspirational mentors and the clients I served. All I could think is: *I was meant for more.*

This was my reality, I worked part-time in healthcare and served clients in my home-based business.

I loved my life. I was fulfilled! I always had new clothes, which helped feel sexy and confident because *I was my own brand.* Serving both roles was a great mix: I was financially sound, I traveled, I met new people, and I helped women feel great about themselves. We can be more than one thing in our life at any given time, and for different reasons.

Many people asked, "Why don't you quit your job?"

My answer was always, "I don't want to!"

And Then, in Steps Life...

In about 2009, my clothing company closed their doors. It shut me down completely. I did not want to move forward with any other company, so I went back to work full-time. I worked hard, climbing the corporate ladder until I got my *dream job*. It was great, until it was not so great. After a while, stress and burnout overshadowed job fulfillment to the point of I was *dying inside*.

During those years, my husband and I did well financially, yet we were operating under the paradigm of scarcity, telling ourselves the story that there was never enough money.

Even though we didn't have much debt, I used retail therapy to fuel my self-worth. I was usually able to keep our credit cards balanced.

And then it happened: the day my world shifted. I was 'restructured' out of my so-called *dream job* after twelve years. Life immediately changed for the better—and for the worse.

For the first time in my life, I was unemployed. I was angry, devastated, relieved and scared all at the same time. When I broke the news to my family, I felt like a failure. I knew I was not going back to management. Although all kinds of emotions existed, I knew this was happening for a reason. I just didn't know what it was at the time.

Operating in shock and fear of the unknown, I moved on like the survivor I am, even though my self-worth was smack-dab at the bottom of perpetually flushing toilet. However, I was more afraid of staying in the slump I was in, than I was of moving forward without having all the answers.

That Pivotal Shift

Twenty days later, I was back at work as a front-line healthcare worker. I also enrolled in a mentorship coaching program. I was a mentor to many in my previous role, so why not choose coaching as a business venture?

The months went on, I picked up a couple of additional healthcare contracts to keep bringing in a wage. In the background, I hired a web design team to brand my coaching business. That way, as soon as I graduated from my coaching program, I would be ready to jump into action and take on clients.

Having no idea how much web design or marketing strategy cost, I trusted the process. I charged everything to my personal credit card. This seemed like a good investment as I began my entrepreneurial journey. After all, clients had to be able to find me online for this business to be a success. Right?

As I networked and met new people, I noticed *everyone* had a coach, some successful people had many coaches for all aspects of their businesses.

I thought this was a very cool idea. I didn't realize it then, but I was seeking validation that I could actually *do* this coaching business online. Plus, on reflection, my self-worth was still missing in action.

My main social media platform is Facebook, which 'watches' what I search for on my device. So, as I googled different types of coaches, my newsfeed was flooded with this information. Down the rabbit hole I went, credit card in hand.

I saw this coach who helps clients make a certain amount of money and I thought, *Wow, I need this because I want to know it all and make some money!* What I didn't realize was that I needed an online presence to succeed—and I only had 200 people on my friends list at the time.

I jumped right in. I signed up for a discovery call, *loved* the coach, and signed up on the spot. I was super stoked to begin building my brand and working with her! I charged the amount to my second personal credit card. She helped me build and brand my business, so I had an amazing website and coaching program.

I was ready! So where were my clients? I made *one* post on Facebook about my business, eagerly awaiting a flood of incoming messages. No one responded. *Not one message!* Shocking, I know! I was hurt and invited myself to a huge pity-party.

Meanwhile, Facebook was serving up all sorts of cool people to follow. In my naiveté, I subscribed to all their email newsletters. I wanted their knowledge because I wanted to learn from the best. I had an inbox full of information and *amazing* offers to the tune of $997 apiece. And all I needed was my credit card! Sadly, I charged many of these courses to my *third* credit card—and never finished them. I felt powerful just because I bought them.

Thinking I was a failure because I didn't have any clients yet, I enrolled in multiple programs for *even more* coaching. I was sure I needed know more, so that people will deem me worthy enough to help them. Or was it so I felt worthy of helping them?

The credit card bills rolled in. All I could see was I was investing in myself and my company. Regardless, I was beginning to feel huge amounts of stress around my bills, as I created more and more debt for myself and my family.

Imagine, having your good self sitting on one shoulder, and your bad self sitting on the other, with your head in the middle. I wanted to learn more, so I could *be* more, knowing the ice was getting thinner and thinner with each credit card transaction. But my course purchasing continued, because I needed to know more to serve my client base. At least that was the story I was telling myself.

My self-worth was all the way down into the sewer now. I had a massive debt load, and *still* no clients. So, what did I do? I accepted more contract work, of course, leaving no room in my schedule to build my business. This pattern carried on for months: coach after coach, with higher and higher ticket items.

However, the knowledge I gained was superb.

I was able to keep making my monthly payments thanks to my healthcare contracts. But because I was working so much to make the money, I had no time to build my business, no clients in year one of my business, *and $80,000 worth of 'investments.'*

In year two of my company, a wonderful woman came along and offered me an opportunity to write in a compilation book. This changed everything for me. I asked my kids what they thought about me writing in this book, as their mom would then be a published author. Their words were, "Go for it. Be *you*."

So, I went for it. I discovered I could write compelling stories, which I was absolutely shocked by. What's more, people liked what I had to say.

This changed the messaging for my coaching business. That meant changing my marketing, and I needed to update my website—*to the tune of another $5000.* Gullible maybe, I trusted him.

The next shocker for me was when Kate Batten, the publisher, reached out to me to ask if I wanted to be mentored in publishing. She saw strengths in my change and project management background, that I loved people, and that I could run projects to a timeline. I also had an aptitude for authentically connecting with people, gaining their trust and could encourage their personal stories to be shared with the world.

The Game Changer

That was the day Follow It Thru Publishing was born. Kate mentored me through the publishing and launching of my own compilation book, where twenty-three people came together to share their stories. This book was a game changer for so many, myself included.

For the first time in two years, I felt like me. I mattered, my co-authors stories mattered and together, we touched people's hearts.

After the compilation launched, my momentum stalled. I was still hooked on my coaching company and put more money into automation. It was like a gambling addiction: just one more spin and I would hit the jackpot. But there was no winning, no escape, no happiness, no fulfillment.

That damn coaching course was never perfect. I realized my demise here was I wanted everything to be *perfect*, hence all the money spent to be viewed a certain way, lest I be judged a loser. And really no one cared.

My coaching course didn't need to be perfect, as nothing ever is. But embracing this reality gave me an idea.

In the fall of 2017, I decided to create another compilation book. It promoted women entrepreneurs who were doing it all and *embracing* the imperfection. Eighteen beautiful souls came together, and we rocked the book *The Real Journey of the Empowered Momboss*. It hit the best seller list right out of the gate. It helped readers get past their overwhelming perception of what others thought of them, and to move forward, to *own* the space to create what they needed in their lives.

It was another pivotal moment in my entrepreneurial journey. I stopped any further development on my website, as I changed direction. I realized I loved my publishing company more than anything and I was going to put all my efforts into it.

At this point, my debtload was upwards of $120,000, and I didn't have a lot to show for it. I did have a lot of knowledge, a whole lot of lessons learned, and the experience to know what to do and *not* to do.

This experience is key: *investments can teach you what to do, and what not to do. Both are incredible learning points to propel you forward.*

Going All In

Back to the point of good debt vs bad debt, I was still on the fence.

As I moved into January 2018, I needed to make a huge decision: *I was either all in or all out.* Enough was enough of investing in a business with no clients. The realization hit like a wrecking ball, as one my editors would say. I knew enough, I had learned enough, and I had been the student long enough. The time had come. My co-authors needed me to show up and be the teacher.

It was in that moment, I knew my business had value; that *I had value.* I had work to do, stories to tell and lives to change. I had come full circle; I needed to realize that my self-love, my talents, and my belief in myself were the most precious assets I had. I needed to reinvent my own story. That was the day, the compilation book, *What's Self Love Got to Do with It* was born, with Dr. Erin Oksol 'attending,' so to speak.

Through publishing the *Momboss* book, I got to know one of my co-authors very well. Jenna Carelli is the firecracker marketing guru that helped me rebrand my publishing business.

The first week of January 2018, I launched my internet radio show, Follow it Thru to your Stellar Life. I hired Jenna Carelli to help me rebrand my company as Heather Andrews. She also built out my publishing websites, adding automation. *I was finally set to grow.*

My then colleague, now business manager, the amazing Carrie Ann Baron, was selling her podcast platform agency. It seemed to be the perfect addition to my corporate offerings, so I bought her out. Where, you ask, did I get the money? Some went on my home equity line of credit. I was also able to get a business loan because I was still working my 'day job,' so I didn't pose a huge risk to the banks.

With no choice left, I invested and made the decision to go *all in.* I have never worked so hard in my life, but I wanted my company to grow and change and succeed so badly, that all I could do was show up, work, and *believe.* Connection to others and building referral partners was key.

By rebranding and investing in the podcast agency to support my vision, growing my team, and hiring a speaker coach, I was $220,000 in at this point. But our revenue was moving ever closer to the six-figure mark. *The shift was happening.*

Throughout 2018, everything that could go wrong, did go wrong. I had clients that did not pay for services rendered. In faith, I took the hit and delivered the product anyway. I paid for coaching that was not delivered. But oh, the lessons I learned. My gut was on fire with red flags most of the time, but I still felt compelled to take on clients. I was on a mission to build my company.

Some decisions helped teach me things, most importantly, to measure growth. We grew too fast, and almost sunk because of it. When a business coach and author of ours stated that growing too fast was almost as detrimental as not having any clients, as either could cause you to go out of business; I learned the power of the pause. We needed to regroup in the last quarter of 2018, as we onboarded thirty-seven new authors, all through referrals—*thirty-seven!*

The books we were publishing were achieving bestselling author status on Amazon, with hundreds of copies being sold.

We were debuted on radio shows, featured in magazines, with speaker opportunities galore.

I spoke over *twenty* times in one year, on stage with the likes of Dr. John D Martini, in Canada and the U.S. The kicker is that regardless of how glam this all sounds, *every month I was hanging on by $10 in the bank.*

Good or bad investments? I will say both. The bad investments changed my life with lessons learned and the establishment of boundaries around invoicing and deliverables.

Trust, Surrender and Elevate

As I reflect on the journey in 2018, I remember my key motivational words being trust, surrender and elevate: trust where you are going, surrender to your mission and elevate others to build your business.

It was a phenomenal year, but in the end, the numbers don't lie. I had hit a six-figure revenue but the amount I owed was too high. I went to the bank, refinancing and getting a huge consolidation loan. I cut up my personal credit cards. I kept my corporate ones. I cashed in some investments to pay off bills, to create space and decrease the stress.

The worst part of all of this was I had built my company and never discussed the amount I spent with my husband. The hardest thing I ever had to do was tell the truth about what I had done to my family financially. I lost control. Yet I was sitting on a company that was flourishing, employing people, had already helped over eighty-five authors share their stories, inspiring thousands of people across the continent.

My authors lives changed, as they were fearful to share their stories. When they became published, their story was freed and so were they. These amazing clients were out to create businesses and build empowering lives. Together we have collaborated and created communities. We have spoken on each other's stages at our events. We text each other in the morning to say good morning. This is the type of stuff that money can't buy.

As the end of December 2018 wrapped up, we had gone from *two* books on Amazon to *twelve*, equaling 95 % business growth. That was with a team of five people standing behind me, Lorraine S, Jen S, Amanda H, Carrie Ann B, and Suzanne S. There is power in knowing that others believe in your mission and vision which is absolutely invaluable and something that can never be bought.

I hit rock bottom that month as the stress was crippling. I had pushed too hard. The universe was nice enough to put me in bed for two weeks with the flu, then I pulled my back and could hardly walk. It was the best Christmas present I could get, as it made me realize my health is my wealth.

If I could not walk, I could not work. That being walking in my job, or in an airport as I traveled to speak and teach for my business. This was more frightening to me than the debt load I carried. It was a plot twist I certainly didn't need. I felt like such a failure, even though my self-worth was the strongest it has ever been, and I was elated with my business.

As I went into January 2019, I was blessed to start the year off by speaking and sharing the stage in Los Angeles and Tampa with my best friend, Dr. Erin Oksol. We met through the power of story in my first compilation book, Obstacles Equal Opportunities. The phrase 'obstacles equal opportunities' is the most truthful statement we have ever created. In every obstacle to date there has been room for learning, patience, tears and opportunities. We have become business partners, best friends and often host events together. Our worlds have aligned, as has the community we have created.

Beyond the money, which ranks up there like oxygen, it is about the people that believe in you and the belief you have in what you are building.

My business has tested me to the brink of losing my home, yet I am loved by my family, supported by team and my clients. I have never believed in anything like I believe in my company, I 'love on' my people like no one else. I believe in the power of story and reinvention because I have lived it. I have always been able to pay my bills, as the money does miraculously appear just when it is needed.

I am happy to say we are setting the stage for 2019 with already record months and our team has *tripled* in size. My team has worked night and day post the power of the pause, to get us aligned with systems, processes and quality assurance and money tracking systems. We know our budgets, forecasts, growth and we have spreadsheets coming our ears. I am held accountable to my team and my family. We have all the payments on a debt repayment plan, and I don't get to do *anything* unless I have cash in the bank. It has been a hell of a lesson. I now know what I can endure.

So, when I say there is good debt, bad debt and the jury is still out that topic. All I know is that if I had to do it all over again, I would only change one thing: I would hang on tight to my self-worth. It is the biggest asset you've got. The number of lives my company has changed is priceless to me and worth every penny I have spent.

Inevitably, the answer to the question of 'good vs bad investments' is: What's Money Got to Do with It? Some things aren't just about the money.

Stay tuned. This journey is not over yet. I've got work to do and stories to share.

"You can only become truly accomplished at something you love. Don't make money your goal. Instead, pursue the things you love doing, and then do them so well that people can't take their eyes off you."

Maya Angelou

A Little Financial Wisdom

The top things I will leave you with are:

1) When you spend money, ask yourself why you need the item you are buying. Check your self-worth scale first.

2) Listen to your intuition. If someone you are hiring sets your gut on fire with the answer 'no,' walk the other way. Immediately. Hire slowly, fire quickly.

3) Build your relationships first, then build your client list. And it's all about relationships.

4) Create a business plan for your business and use it as your guide. Revisit, and update it regularly.

5) Don't max out personal credit cards, it is a *bitch* to pay them back.

6) Credit is a great thing, depending how it is used.

7) Following your passion and purpose is a beautiful thing—just make sure you can fund it. Keep your job and build your company slowly.

8) Hire your experts to help you with your business set up and ongoing financial numbers. Keep your business accounts separate from your personal ones. Consult your financial advisors, accountants and banks to seek options.

9) Have a financial date night. Put the topic on the table as there are many facets to it. Be truthful about what you do.

10) Make informed decisions. There is no quick road to riches. You need to do the work.

Aha Moments and Self Reflections

Note your Thoughts

Conclusion

In the end, money is all about empowerment. It's about creating the freedom to pursue what you hold dear, what you value, *what you love*.

As we come to the end of our *What's Money Got to Do with It* journey together, we hope you've been able to latch on to a few golden nuggets of advice that will serve you as your own financial story unfolds.

Now it's time to put all these strategies, tactics and tools to work for *you*, as you engineer your new money story. It's time to put all your proverbial chips on the table, assess all your options, and address your issues. It's time to get real and get down-right honest about your financial situation—whatever state it happens to be in.

Getting back into the black isn't going to be easy. You didn't get into debt overnight, and you aren't likely to get out of it overnight either. (As much as many of us would like it to be, winning the lottery isn't a solid financial strategy!)

Taking action is key. While none of us plan to let our debt get out of control, having a pragmatic, realistic plan to get *out* of debt is critical. Being the architect of your financial future is empowering in itself, regardless of how long it's going to take, or how much you may have to let go of short-term to get to where you want to be at the end of the long game.

The relief I felt when I finally confronted my spending and credit card bills was like a spiritual revelation. The sheer weight of those shiny little cards in your pocket is heavier than gold bullion. The burden of carrying that financial weight around—day-in, day-out, without an offloading strategy—is mentally, physically and emotionally crippling.

And you *will* get to the end of the long game. Throughout *What's Money Got to Do with It*, we have focused on how our personal relationships with money had to change in order for many of us to overcome the barriers to our financial success. Just because you had one money story in the past, doesn't mean that's the only money story you're 'allowed' to have. You can start to create a better financial future by openly expressing where you want to be in the end. Let that vision be your guide. Shift your money mindset to one of wealth rather than one of scarcity.

The good news is, you don't have to do all this on your own. Many of the co-authors in this book offer services to help you get on your way. Their expert knowledge and experience is there to help you to plot your course, to furnish you with all the tools and strategies you need to help you develop your financial dexterity, and to advise you of other products and services that may suit your individual situation.

Finally, discover the riches in the lesson. As hard as it may seem at the time, our financial trials teach us what we should, or should not, do the next time a similar situation materializes. Be thankful for all you've learned along the way. Wisdom is wealth well earned.

Walk tall, my friends. You've earned it.

I Belong Bags

By Founder Tanya Forbes

As of June 2018, there were 10,647 Alberta children and youth receiving Child Intervention Services. This was a 2% increase from the previous year. Of that number, 7423 of these children were children placed directly in care outside the home and 3842 were placed in foster care.

Did you know that children in crisis apprehended from their homes for their own protection usually leave with only the clothes on their backs? If they are afforded the opportunity to take anything, they are given a trash bag to collect it in and this trash bag becomes their luggage to hold their most treasured belongings they will drag from home to home as they get moved around.

To me, this sends a pretty damaging psychological message to a child. We as humans are pre-wired to make all kinds of meaning out of circumstances in our lives. These meanings we attach to our self-worth in the world—sometimes it's empowering and sometimes it's damaging. Now imagine a child who has just been removed from their home because of a traumatic event, abuse, neglect or worse and you add to that this meaning making trash bag moment. What kind of message would this imbed in the mind of a child? 'Disposable' comes to mind. "I'm garbage", "nobody wants me". You can imagine the damage this is doing already right?

And so, this child isn't really dragging a trash bag full of their belongings anymore, they are dragging this newly created identity and self-worth that was born out of tragedy and trauma when they were maybe eight years old. What are the chances of this child, who already has a difficult and uncertain battle ahead of them, developing into happy and productive members of our community, dragging this "trash bag" of self-worth with them into every life situation and relationship going forward?

We know that early traumatic child experiences and toxic stress can change the developing architecture of the brain. This change can negatively affect learning and mental and physical health outcomes throughout a child's life. The good news is that healthy bonds with caregivers and peers and strong community supports will help to buffer the effects of toxic stress experienced by children in crisis. It will help to build a healthy brain foundation that is critical for learning and development into happy and productive members of society. I feel it is up to us as a community to ensure that these kids have the healthy and nurturing experiences they need to succeed through their journey.

To change this trash bag moment for a child in crisis, I founded the organization, I Belong Bags, where we restore dignity, self-worth, and a sense of belonging to a child in crisis. To be a part of this amazing community of supporting these children, please visit: https://www.facebook.com/ibelongbags/ or contact tanyaforbes@shaw.ca

Statistics from humanservices.alberta.ca

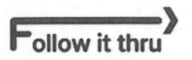

Follow it thru

The question remains the same at the end of the book as it did in the beginning—What's Money Got to Do with It?

My answer is still everything. However, several things have changed since the beginning of the book, you have many different tools strategies and are no longer alone. You have read how your money story can change once you are ready to embrace a new one.

After all the 'aha' moments and self-reflective journaling, my question for you is, are you ready to act? You have read it here. Action creates change.

A few questions you may want to ask yourself are:

Are you feeling like your finances are out of control?

Do you your finances keep you up at night?

Are you maxed out?

Are you willing to examine and see what you can do differently?

Are you willing to be honest with yourself about your money and create a budget?

If your finances are out of control, chances are there are other aspects that are too?

How did this happen? If money were a simple mathematical equation without life happening, chances are we would all be rich. As we know, life happens! Most of the time it requires money to fix issue.

This book was created to bring open and honest conversations to the table about money and yes, it is scary. You are not alone.

I encourage you to stop for a moment and think about the feelings that occurred as you read the stories in this book and reflected on your own lessons learned and mindset tips. If you find yourself saying, "This is too hard" or "I can't do it by myself," then my answer is that you are not meant to do it on your own.

As a visibility strategist, publisher, and having lived my own self-worth reinvention, along with investing in my own company I can tell you that there is a different way! There is a way for you to get a grip on the chaos, harness your finances, change your money mindset, and restore your financial future.

Is it easy? Maybe probably not.

Does it take work? Yes

Does it take patience? Yes

Worth it? YES—PRICELESS

The choice is yours!

You can do it by asking for support from your loved ones or friends.

It might even involve hiring a mentor or enrolling in a course

You can reach out to the co-authors and their expertise to help you that is why they wrote this book, so you are not alone on your financial journey.

You can join our Facebook group and become part of a community of people just like you.

https://www.facebook.com/groups/GetYouVisible/

I have been where you are, and I understand. There is a different path for you.

Let's talk!

Heather Andrews

https://followitthru.as.me/tellyourstory

Do You Dream of Being a Published Author?

The best part of what I do is bringing people together to write, share, and inspire those that may feel alone or in need of healing. Your story could help to heal others.

My team will guide you through the writing process, so your idea can become a reality to be shared on worldwide distribution channels.

A book has been referenced as an authority piece for centuries and is known to be one of the best ways to gain instant credibility and visibility with clients in the online and offline space.

If you have a story to share and want to become a published author or co-author in a collaborative, then let's talk.

Book your complimentary call with me.

https://followitthru.as.me/tellyourstory

Here's to your story and someone waiting to read it.

Heather

https://www.facebook.com/groups/GetYouVisible/